← Travel Guide →
to
Port Charles

When to Go, Where to Live, Who to Love,
and Who to Never, Ever Cross
in America's Most Dramatic City

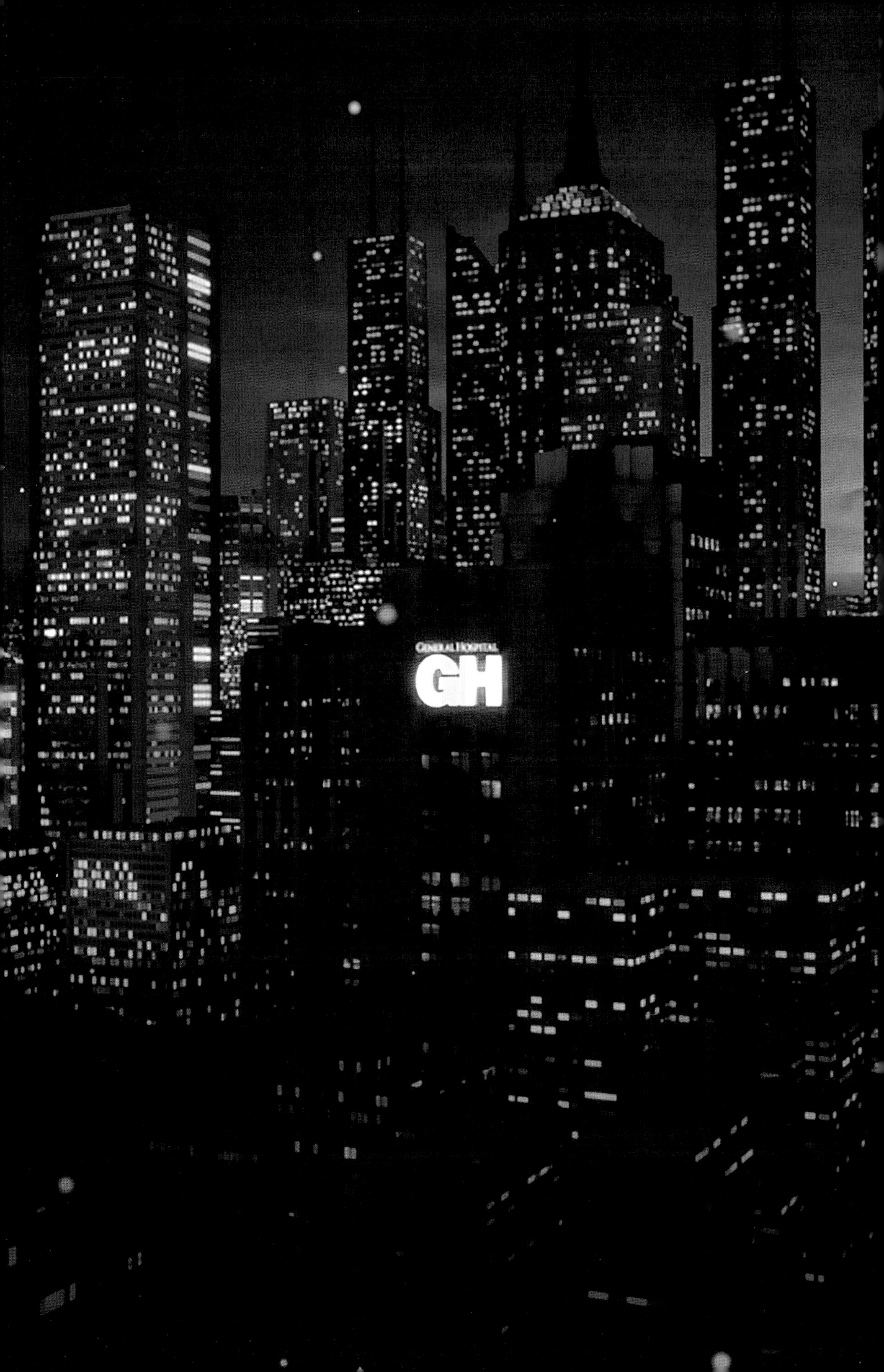
GENERAL HOSPITAL
GH

← Travel Guide → to Port Charles

*When to Go, Where to Live, Who to Love,
and Who to Never, Ever Cross
in America's Most Dramatic City*

Lucy Coe

KINGSWELL

LOS ANGELES • NEW YORK

Photo credits:
ABC/Ron Tom: pages, 43, 46, 78-79, 88-89, 95. ABC/Rick Rowell: page 149. All other set photos courtesy of ABC.
Images provided by Alamy Stock Photo: 2-3 Brilt / Alamy Stock Photo; 4-5 Taina Sohlman / Alamy Stock Photo; 4-5
Michael Burrell / Alamy Stock Photo; 6 Blend Images / Alamy Stock Photo; 6 Elena Elisseeva / Alamy Stock Photo;
10-11 picturesbyrob / Alamy Stock Photo; 12 Elena Elisseeva / Alamy Stock Photo; 21 Björn Wylezich / Alamy Stock
Photo; 33 Kzenon / Alamy Stock Photo; 36-37 Ron Hayes / Stockimo / Alamy Stock Photo; 54-55 GoHollywood /
Alamy Stock Photo; 188 Gaertner / Alamy Stock Photo.
All other stock images from Purestock.

Note from Editor: Port Charles is a fictional city where General Hospital, the ABC show is located.

For information address Kingswell,
1200 Grand Central Avenue, Glendale, California 91201.

Editorial Director: Wendy Lefkon
Executive Editor: Laura Hopper
Designed by Julie Rose

ISBN 978-1-368-01937-8
FAC-038091-18278

Printed in the United States of America
First Paperback Edition, November 2018
1 3 5 7 9 10 8 6 4 2

Visit www.disneybooks.com

This book is . . .

NOT for Kevin O'Connor . . .
the first and last drip for whom I'd ever forswear makeup and high heels.

NOT for Jake Meyer . . .
who had the decency to take me to Lamaze class, but the nerve
to hold it against me. I didn't get pregnant by myself, Jake!

NOT for Tony Jones . . .
who was not driven to blindness by marriage to moi! He needed brain surgery!

NOT for Scott Baldwin . . .
who was too cheap to buy me diamonds.

NOT for Victor Jerome . . .
who wasn't too cheap to buy me diamonds,
but was too much a crime boss for me to accept them.

NOT for Alan Quartermaine . . .
who fought his sister for control of the family company all his life,
but had the gall to tell me I was greedy! Me!

NOT for Damian Smith . . .
who probably wishes he'd never been a betting man.

NOT for Kevin Collins . . .
who always was too good for the likes of me anyway.

NOT for Tom Hardy or Greg Bennett or Richard Halifax or
Rex Stanton or Ian Thornhart or any of the other louses
I've ever had the misfortune to cross paths with. . . .

This book isn't for any ex-husband, ex-boyfriend, ex-crush, or ex-romance.
This book is for the person who made me the successful, brilliant, clever,
woman/mother/cosmetics maven/top real estate broker I am today.

This book is for me.

AN INTRO BY LUCY COE

*B*ut first! A little about your guide, your reliable narrator, little ol' me. . . .

My first bra was a push-up. I purchased it with the money I'd scrimped sweeping the floors at Cute-icles, the local beauty salon run by my aunt Charlene. I was twelve.

Never mind that there wasn't anything to push up at the time. It was an aspirational purchase. "If I buy it," I dreamed, "they will come." Charlene walked in on me modeling it for the flimsy full-length mirror in my closet. She didn't bat a single swooping eyelash.

"Don't look too close, Sugar," she drawled—back then she had a twang like a tightrope. "You might just see something you don't like."

I paid her no mind. "You're jealous," I called to her back as she swished out with a hamper full of my skivvies. "Besides, this mirror's not gonna look at itself." I went right on admiring. If I didn't do it, who would? Back then I was elbows and knees for days. The only person I could count on to see through the baby fat to the beauty revving up beneath was me.

Or so I thought. Perhaps if I'd given my aunt proper credit, I might have played it cool and spared myself the tumult to come. You see, Charlene had a knack for sizing people up—not to mention shaking them down. Legend had it she was known to many a riverboat casino bouncer. Scads of eligible poker-playing bachelors were said to have lost their hearts to Charlene—and then their wallets. She was hip to trouble because she'd been trouble herself! And she knew it thrived in girls whose appetites outstripped what was on offer in certain backwoods Texas towns.

Towns like mine. Girls like me.

My hometown was so dull even dust knew better than to settle there. A girl's Friday night pickings were slim and bleak: you could do-si-do your way through the weekly square dance in the Methodist church's basement, gouge your eyes out at the high school football game, or throw yourself into the scrum of teenaged hormones frothing in the parking lot behind the Dairy Queen.

Suffice it to say, you wouldn't catch me dead in gingham, and football held all the allure of a career in the library sciences. Note: as you'll later learn, this assessment would come back to haunt me.

I was left with no choice but to spend my Friday nights checking out what was on offer at the Dairy Queen—and in case you haven't gotten the hint, Dear Reader, Blizzards were *not* on my menu. My pubescent prayers were answered by my four-teenth birthday when I came into a body with more curves than a can of worms. Who was I to let such gifts go to waste?

So, Aunt Charlene sat my parents down one afternoon and delivered the bad news—their darling little Lucy was *fast*. "That girl has a strut sitting down, Sis." Of *course* I eavesdropped! "And if you're not careful, she'll be sitting on a nest quicker than a sneeze through a screen door!"

My parents thought little of Charlene's warning. She'd put on airs since her three-month stint as a backup dancer in Branson; to them, she was citi-fied and given to embellishment. They would brook no criticism of me, the apple of their eye—but the image of their little girl was clouded by cataracts. Who knows how my life might've turned out if they had only heeded Charlene's warning and brought me to heel before that fateful church service? While the congregation was singing the good lord's praises, I was in the Bible study room, hunkered down with a hunky cowboy singing notes few but the heathen could hear.

Put another way, we weren't studying the Bible, we were studying each other . . . in the biblical style.

Put yet another way, we were going at it—until the pastor's wife found us out, alerted by sounds she previously only dreamed of making.

The congregation swooned, Charlene crowed, my parents cried, and I packed my bags. It was exile for me, banishment somewhere far enough away that no one would know my shame. I was to eke out my high school years in an all-girls school, doing my

darndest to take Charlene's parting words to heart. "I bet you think you're being taught a lesson, don't you, darlin'."

"Have you seen the uniforms they wear at this school?!" I wailed. I was a wailer, then. "Brillo has a higher thread count!"

Charlene reeled me in close and purred, "Don't you remember *The Sound of Music*? When life hands you drapes, sew 'em into rompers. You can show up at that school trailing your trash behind you or you can arrive with a new look and a new identity to go along with it. This could be the best thing to ever happen to you. It's your ticket out of here. And if you're smart, you'll stay out. There's nothing but kitchens and nurseries here for you, Lucy. You've got more rooms in you than that."

And so began my second great transformation—not a transformation that was biologically thrust upon me but one I undertook of my own free will. There would be many more revamps in my future, but this one was by far the most important; it's the one that got the jewel-encrusted ball rolling on all those yet to come. For it was there at the Scath-ington School for Wayward Girls in rural Beecher's Corners, New York, that I developed the quali-ties required to remake myself as circumstances warranted. Among them: grit, patience, and the confidence to buck conventional wisdom.

Don't believe me? Just wait until next year when I single-handedly bring back the patchwork peasant skirt. Wearable quilts will be hot again. You heard it here first.

But the most important trait with which I escaped from Scathington's was unswerving faith in myself. It would've been easy to succumb to my teachers' casually cruel insistence that we students would never amount to much. They thought they were doing us a favor, managing our expectations. Scathington's was built to refine one's manners and dull one's dreams, its graduates meant to achieve little more than matrimony and motherhood. And though I did learn that marriage has its uses (I stopped counting after my fifth wedding), I was determined to ask more of myself. Charlene was right: my possibilities were endless, and tantalizingly close at hand . . . so close, in fact, that I could practically see them every night after lights out. All I had to do was turn over in bed and turn my gaze out the window across Scathington's grounds and over the cornfields to the faint glow of a certain metropolis just an hour's drive to the north, a place teeming with mystery and potential, a place a wayward girl could reinvent herself over and over again until she shaped the version of herself that fit to a tee.

I knew I wouldn't have the materials to tailor the right me among the clucking matrons back home or in Texas—or wedded to some stale suit in the suburbs, as Scathington's would have of me. But that city held everything I'd need to fashion myself into the bust-a-mover-and-shaker I was destined to become.

So, as soon as I received my walking papers from Scathington's, I walked to the curb and thumbed a ride to that city on the shining shores of Lake Ontario . . .

. . . Port Charles!

Okay, I know what you're thinking.

Huh?

"But Lucy, you were a young woman on the move! A hot number with ambition and legs—and smarts to spare! Why not hitch your wagon to a star in New York City?" What was I, made of money?

"Los Angeles, then!" The smog! The people!

"Even Cleveland!" Their river was on fire back then, people! The EPA was created on account of Cleveland!

Yes, there were other cities I might've made my way to. There was Rochester to the east and Buffalo to the west. But as far as I was concerned, the only things Buffalo had in abundance were lake-effect snow and heartache; and I associated Rochester with *Jane Eyre*, a book I picked up and put down a thousand times, never making it past the part with Brocklehurst (because that broken slate just reminded me of all the ways I'd disappointed my parents).

Relocating to Buffalo or Rochester also would've required bus fare, and as hinted at above, I was no longer flat-chested—just flat broke.

Are you getting the wrong idea, Dear Reader? Are you wondering just what sort

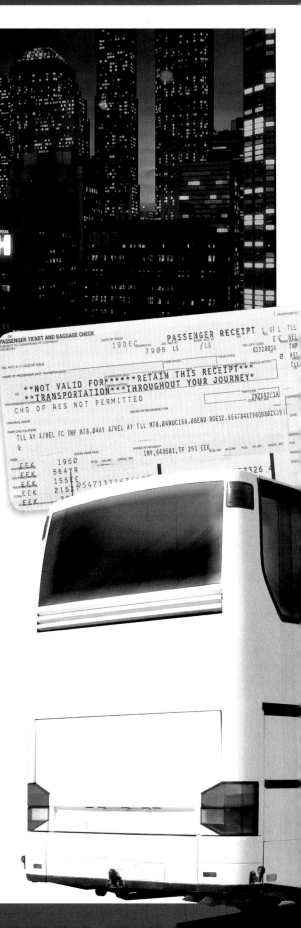

of cheerleader I can be for Port Charles if I didn't seek out this city so much as land in it? It's a good question, to which I offer this answer: There's no zeal like the zeal of the converted, and baby, I can preach.

At first glance, Port Charles might seem like your typical western New York state city. But scratch the surface and I know you'll find what I have: a vibrant, diverse, cosmopolitan community positively reeking of excitement, opportunity, and mouthwatering BLTs. We have big business in ELQ and Cassadine Industries! Just don't ask me what they do, or make, or provide because I have no idea. We're honing the cutting edge of fashion and art and research into diseases you've never heard of and pray you never get!

All that work making you hungry and dull? We've got a smorgasbord full of foreign and native culinary delights on tap, and all the entertainment you'll ever need with some world-class people watching! Seriously, who needs movies or TV when you can drop by our city's General Hospital for your flu shot only to stumble upon a ring of embryo thieves? Grab a drink at one of our watering holes and you just may find yourself audience to the airing out of a bigamist's secret sex soiree! Attend a charity gala at gothic Wyndemere Castle and you could meet your very own prince—just steer clear of turrets and parapets . . . and Greco-Russian, dagger-wielding grandmothers.

In Port Charles you're as likely to encounter a den of not-so-secret agents as you are a gold-hearted, gun-toting "coffee importer." You may strike it rich peddling pickle relish or platinum records. You could find love on a bungee jump over Blackstone Canyon or waltzing the marbled perfume aisles of Wyndham's, our legendary department store/handy hideout.

But as they say about the lottery, you can't win it if you don't play. You won't do any of it if you aren't here. And your chances of hitting it big are a lot better in Port Charles than they are with a liquor store scratch-off.

So get cozy and get cracking. Flip these pages and discover much of what Port Charles has to offer. Here you'll find the lowdown on the history of our fair (if not always just) city—though not only from *moi*. I've enlisted contributions from a slew of friends and neighbors all with their own unique take on where to settle, what to eat, how to have fun, whom to befriend, and whom to avoid. (Let us be real, every city has 'em.) Please don't be put off by some of the more, er, evocative tidbits you'll find within. My pesky editor insists on "full transparency" about Port Charles's rather colorful history. (Editor's note: Consider that a disclaimer. It's not our fault if you move to Port Charles and get caught up in a mob war.)

Sure, we experience the occasional natural disaster, or plague, or vampire scare. But isn't that the stuff of life?

Come visit Port Charles. Let us be your guides. I promise the experience will change you for the better or your money back, guaranteed! (Editor's note: That statement does not constitute a legally binding contract.) Coming here changed me! Many times, in fact! Granted, some of the more positive changes required a year or ten to take—but hey, not every metamorphosis may be attained with a simple wardrobe adjustment. If you seek a little *va-va-va-voom*, make Port Charles your destination. It's the push-up bra for life.

Lucy Coe

Port Charles is the seat of Eerie County (not to be confused with the Erie County to the west; some explorer's idea of a joke), tucked midway between Buffalo and Rochester and situated on the southern shore of Lake Ontario, the smallest—but loveliest—of the Great Lakes.

Now don't go @ing me, Clevelanders and Kenoshans! Lakes Erie and Michigan have their qualities, but Ontario's beauty is objective truth. Go on, ask any mirror, mirror. If you refuse to believe me, if you demand rock solid evidence, you can either book an aerial tour or simply seek out a scenic overlook from the

highest point around, Cedar Mountain. Just hop in your car or hire one from Slick's Taxi Service[1] and take Route 31 south for ten miles out of the city. Look for the pretty little turnoff just after the exit for Branford. Park your car and look for a signpost that'll point you to a nature path up the peak. It's a bit of a hike, so leave your Cartullo heels in the car, ladies.

Fifteen minutes of mild- to moderate-cardio later, you'll arrive at a pedestrian path lining the Blackstone Bridge. The bridge lassoes a canyon of the same name that's carved into the side of the mountain. From its verticals, you'll enjoy a sweeping vista of the city; spot

[1] Says Laura W, "Whether I'm late for my flight to Cassadine Island or hot on the trail of a terrifically ugly statue that just may hold the key to climate change, Slick's Taxi Service provides my backup wheels of choice! Who needs a ride app when you've got Slick's? Their drivers are prompt and knowledgeable; they know all the shortcuts—and their prices are cut-rate. The offices of Slick's Taxi Service are located at 525 Wharf Street. Call 716-555-TAXI to open an account today! Mention coupon code "Ice Princess" for 10 percent off your first ride!

the spire of ELQ Tower; the five-star restaurant atop the Metro Court Hotel; and the lake just beyond. Hand to God, there exists no bluer a blue than the waters of Lake Ontario—except perchance the blue eyes of a certain mister known to frequent the Blackstone Bridge.[2] If you're looking for unrequited love, you could do worse than to try your luck at Blackstone. Tall, dark, black-T-shirt, and leather-jacket–clad strangers abound.

If you're looking to add more mystery and intrigue to your life, be sure to bring some binoculars and train your eye on the Charles River below. Follow its path from the canyon north to the suburbs and through the city, where it feeds into the lake, then set your sights a mile from the mouth and onto the swirl of mists veiling spooky Spoon Island. It was there on that rocky spit late in 1681 that the explorer Gaspard Charles tumbled off his longboat, ralphed up his vittles, and claimed the area for the French. Charles had been sent by King Louis XIV to follow up on predecessor Samuel de Champlain's efforts to seek out a route to the Pacific.

To our great fortune, Charles turned out to be something of a homebody. He abandoned his mission upon catching sight of the Ontario

Ontario's beauty is objective truth

[2] Says Jason M, "Sometimes at night I ride my motorcycle out to Blackstone. It's a pretty nice spot. I like to look down at the city and be by myself and think. Trouble is, I keep running into people there. I think I need to find a new spot. When asked to comment, Jason's good friend Robin S once stated, "We'll still find you."

dunes, which so reminded him of his home back in Normandy. He fell crazy in love and announced to his astonished crew that their voyage was over. Flag planted, Charlesiana was born.

And then he promptly died.

History tells us Charles had a stubborn streak. Common sense tells us he was an arrogant nincompoop. He did not take to heart warnings from a friendly group of Seneca natives who spoke of strange sounds and an unearthly glow that sometimes wafted across the shore from the island; nor did he mind the common sense advice of his wife, Marie, who insisted they lacked the provisions to withstand the coming winter and ought to decamp for the mainland where their odds of survival were slim, not slim to none. Charles insisted he would make do on his island redoubt, even after his crew and Marie packed up their leather stockings and headed for safety across the water; even as his stores dwindled; even as the lake-effect snow piled up. After the spring thaw a search party set out to rescue Charles; but the island was empty. He was nowhere to be found. The only traces left of Charles were the remnants of his rickety lean-to and his dinghy, into which was carved a single, peculiar word: "Lumina."[3]

Marie carried on in his absence, assumed leadership of the party, and sent for settlers, helping to establish a working colony, thus earning her widespread respect and admiration—not to mention numerous offers of marriage. She declined them all, opting instead to end the Charles line in favor of

maintaining her independence and her name, lending it only to the settlement that became the Port Charles we know and love today.

Now look off to the west and you'll behold a great forested wilderness known as the Pine Barrens. A dedicated state nature and historic preserve, the Pine Barrens are a perfect spot for bird-watching, a quiet nature walk, restful reflection, and picturesque picnics . . . as well as the discreet disposal of victims of mob violence.[4] Local lore suggests[5] the lonely

---

[3] Says Anna D in her delightful British accent, "Don't ahsk me."

[4] Says Sonny C, "No comment."

[5] Says Johnny Z, "It's not lore, it's the truth! Sonny Corinthos and his flunky Jason Morgan buried my sister out there!"

backcountry is a favorite dumping ground for ne'er-do-wells[6] across the region eager to rid themselves of evidence, enemies—and eyewitnesses. So if you go, bring a map, pack a lunch, and if you hear the telltale sound of grave-digging, turn around and run—don't walk—the other way.[7]

Round out your survey of Port Charles and its surroundings with a gander to its east and south. Just a hop, skip, and a jump from the center of the city you'll find the bedroom community of Branford. Mostly a commuter town, Branford is rather unremarkable in comparison to its much larger cousin—which is just the way its residents like it. "We hereabouts much prefer quiet and a leisurely pace to the hustle and bustle of Port Charles," says Branford's unofficial historian, Gene Goldbury. "A lot of city people barely know we exist," he reckons, "which is not to say we don't have our attractions.

[6] Says attorney Diane M, "My client categorically denies the insinuation that he was involved in any way, shape, or form in the death and/or burial of Claudia Zacchara. My client is a pillar of the community, a philanthropist, a simple coffee importer."

[7] Editor's note: Much more on the subject of crime is sprinkled throughout these pages. See for instance one of our walking tours, "A Mosey with the Mob."

"If you're looking to wet your whistle with a limited craft batch," Goldbury adds, "you could do worse than stop in at a certain out-of-the-way spot in our little town." Gene is referring to the eponymously named Gene's Branford Beer Garden,[8] where locals rub elbows with visitors[9] looking to quench their thirst[10]—or just to escape it all.[11]

A good strong squint to the south and you may just make out the rustic hamlet of Beecher's Corners, some seventy-five miles distant. Port Charlesers tend to overlook Beecher's Corners, blowing by on their way to the larger hub of Fair Oaks further on. Dear Reader, I double-dog dare you not to repeat their mistake! To the untrained eye the farming community of Beecher's Corners may amount to little more than a main street and a bus stop.

But there's much more to Port Charles's breadbasket than that. Ask anyone in Clem's General Store or Mom and Pop Calhoun's Diner about Lloyd and Lucy[12] Johnson—then look for a gleam in their eye. Lloyd and Lucy were the aliases for two of Port Charles's

. . . Luke and Laura landed ❧ in Beecher's Corners ❧ while on the run . . .

[8] Gene's Branford Beer Garden is located at 17 Liftbridge Lane in Branford. Call 716-555-4516 to hear about the day's menu.

[9] Says Alexis D, "Gene's customers can generally drink in peace and privacy, undisturbed by a tactful staff trained to keep its distance. The same cannot be said for certain ex-husbands who may tail their former spouses and stick their noses into business not their own. I can no longer speak to the variety and quality of the beer menu, but it was without equal during the period when I was a faithful customer."

[10] Says Julian J, "I recommend parking on the street. The lot is not well lit, and I still bear the tire tracks on my back to prove it."

[11] Says Alexis D, "It was an accident. Get over it!"

[12] Lucy's note: No relation.

most celebrated citizens: Luke Spencer and Laura Collins (née Spencer née Baldwin née Webber). Back in 1980, Luke and Laura landed in Beecher's Corners while on the run from mob boss Frank Smith's hired goons. They might have been caught and rubbed out—if not for the abundant local hospitality.[13]

And thank goodness for that! For although Port Charles had already been humming along for some two hundred years, it was the adventures of Luke Spencer and Laura Webber that truly put it on the map.[14] There are even those who say that it was only through their efforts that Port Charles exists at all![15] Think about it: if Luke and Laura hadn't fallen in love, the world as we know it might have come to a very chilling end. . . .[16]

[13] Editor's note: There's more to learn about on the subject of Beecher's Corners and other points of interest located outside Port Charles proper. For more information, please see the section entitled "Further Afield."

[14] Editor's note: For more on Luke and Laura's *high* jinks, see our walking tour, "Saunter and Save the World."

[15] Editor's note: Sorry, me again. Claims about the nature and extent of Luke and Laura's early exploits are corroborated by news accounts of the time; still, details are vague and far-fetched. Readers are advised to approach these claims with a skeptical eye.

[16] Lucy's note: Skeptical eye my foot! I have it direct from the mouth of Luke Spencer himself! And what a mouth it is. . . .

Every now and then I hear the whispers of certain visitors to Port Charles who dare declare they'll not soon return. It's not because of the people, not because of the food—but because of the climate! It's true that nobody's going to hit the jackpot farming sunshine in western New York, and some smarty-pants snigger that our four seasons are winter, slush, bummer, and flu. I refused to believe anyone would turn down an opportunity to experience all that we have to offer based on some forty-year-old bad press![17] But then the opportunity to pen this book came along and I figured I ought to make an effort[18]

THROUGH THE YEAR

to learn the truth. So, I surveyed some former colleagues in the style business, knowing they would give it to me straight. Well the hags gave it to me, all right—right in the kisser!

"Lucy, darling, Port Charles is so many things . . ." sniffs the wicked witch of Pine Valley, former Enchantment cosmetics maven Erica Kane. "It's home to such unique characters, setting for so many colorful stories, birthplace to an array of eyebrow-raising fashions—like that oh-so-memorable red satin dress you wore to your wedding to Alan Quartermaine! The skintight number? With the hat? The one that might double as a flotation device?"[19] It was couture! It was also a million years ago, and it wasn't my fault! I would never choose to wear crimson to my own wedding! I was sent the wrong dress and there was no time to find a replacement! It was either make do with what I had or cobble something together from Aunt Charlene's wardrobe of rhinestones and shawls! But church lady chic just would not do. So, I made do!

[17] Editor's note: See below.
[18] Editor's note: A token effort.
[19] Editor's note: A *Crimson Magazine* retrospective of 1990s avant-garde wedding dresses labeled it the "haute mess of the century."

"Of course you did, Lucy." Erica is as soothing as an air-raid siren. "That's what you do in Port Charles—you make do. But honey, here's the problem: I simply can do better. And I most definitely don't do drear."

I was sure a polymath-like-doctor-turned-publisher-turned-ambassador-turned-cosmetics-maven-turned-Senator Dorian Lord of Llanview, PA, would see the sterling silver lining in Port Charles's occasional clouds. But even she turned up her nose at "That gelid, sunless bog? Sorry, not sorry, Lucy—I wouldn't step into Port Charles with Todd Manning's foot!"

Heed not their words, Intrepid Traveler! After all, their hometowns of Pine Valley and Llanview are the last two stops on the train

to Nowheresville. And I ought to have known better than ask their opinion. Do remember, Erica once ran away to become a Vegas showgirl, and nobody rocks prison-denim blue like former death row inmate Dorian Lord. Let she who has not made a misstep cast the first stiletto!

They can stay and rot in their backwater burgs for all I care. Take it from me, Dear Reader, Port Charles may occasionally suffer from a little[20] notoriety, but there's one thing about it that's pretty darn normal: the weather. Take a look at the almanac and you'll see that we enjoy a typically sultry, humid summer, followed by a crisp autumn that's perfect for pumpkin-patch romps and scenic fall-foliage tours.

But they were right about our winters. Our winters are hell on earth.

We get snow. We get ice. We get snow *and* ice at the same time, from all directions: north, south, east, west, up AND down; sometimes all at once. We get bluster and blizzards and ice storms and the dreaded lake-effect snow. There's early frost, black frost, permafrost, and hoarfrost; come to think of it, there's regular frost, too. We don't lack for gales, drafts, and drear; some etymologists suggest the term "wintry mix" was first coined by the bartender in the old Port Charles Hotel.

We get snow. We get ice. We get snow and ice at the same time.

If you've elected to visit our fair but frigid city in the months of December, January, or February, you will find yourself smack-dab in the eye of a vast polar vortex. But from the inside of a ski lodge on Cedar Mountain, or a hot tub sipping a hot toddy, it's actually really quite pretty! And when the planet finally reorients itself come spring, we pop off like nobody's business. So, you see, it's a perfectly ordinary climate for a community positioned on the 43rd parallel.

Except for the once-in-a-lifetime,[21] life-threatening freak midsummer blizzard.

Okay, bear with me. I know how that reads. But it really did happen![22] No, I was not there to feel it happen with my own dry skin, but any number of longtime residents will attest to the fact that in August of 1981 Port Charles endured an honest-to-God blizzard . . . made up entirely of artificial snow.

"*Carbonic* snow," growls Luke Spencer, "not to be confused with the stuff you find on the bunny slopes." He spoke to me from the Amsterdam canal house in which he currently hides from Port Charles's most infamous medusa, Tracy Quartermaine. "Those bureaucrats at the WSB[23] have tried to keep the truth under wraps for almost forty years, threatening me with this, that, and the

---

[20] Editor's note: Just a little?

[21] Says Luke S, "Though not for a certain dragon lady's lack of trying."

[22] Editor's note: This is one of those instances in which we will present eyewitness accounts along with what facts we are in possession and allow the reader to draw his or her own conclusions.

[23] World Security Bureau. Yes, it is a thing, an international organization designed to protect the planet from the more dastardly menaces. For more, please see enjoy our tour, "A Walkabout with the WSB."

other—but I'm finally too old and too ornery to pay them any mind. Carbonic snow is real! Ask my sister."[24]

"It's true," Bobbie Spencer tells me with that totally put-on, breathy, Betty Boop voice that acts like a dog whistle to lesser evolved men. "I left for work one day and the temperature had dropped from ninety-eight to fifty-five overnight! It lost another ten degrees after that. As the sun rose, the temperature fell in equal measure. Nobody could understand it." Personally I'm not surprised Bobbie couldn't understand it. She wouldn't have survived a single semester at Scathington's.

"It's said it all started with my husband Alan's cousin, Alexandria," opines General Hospital's chief of staff Monica Quartermaine. "She'd arranged to have shipped to Port Charles what was thought to be the largest uncut diamond in the world—the Ice Princess. Painted it black for some ungodly reason. Ugliest damn thing I'd ever seen, and that includes witnessing my sister-in-law, Tracy, sweatin' to the oldies."

Luke told me that the Ice Princess was no ordinary hunk of rock on a pedestal. "Few knew it at the time, but that minx Alexandria and her partner-in-mad-science, one James Duvall, had been cooking up some chemistry voodoo in their spare time—a formula to manufacture synthetic diamonds.[25] The recipe was secreted away in the Ice Princess's base."

Everyone wanted the Ice Princess! Alexandria's Uncle Edward was out to get it for himself, Alexandria wanted her formula back, Luke wanted to cash it in for a tidy sum . . . but a mysterious stranger named Tony Castle appeared to have the inside track. It seemed like the only people who weren't interested in the Ice Princess were those fortunate enough to have good taste! Says that boss Aussie, agent Robert Scorpio of the WSB, "It had vanished from Alexandria's possession only to reappear in the hands of a slightly unsophisticated[26] social climber named Emma Lutz, who in turn donated it to Lila Quartermaine's art auction benefitting General Hospital.

A lot of folks attended that auction, intending to get the Ice Princess for themselves—or, in my case, for the WSB and the greater good. But somebody cut the power, and by the time the lights came back on it had disappeared again."

"Alexandria got it back eventually and we learned she was really in cahoots with Tony Castle; whose last name was actually Cassadine," Luke told me, "of the Greco-Russian dynasty of demons."

"Tony was a dreamboat," swoons actress-turned-television anchor Tiffany Hill.[27] "All the Cassadine men were. His brother,

> *. . . Ice Princess was no ordinary hunk of rock on a pedestal*

---

[24] Editor's note: In fact-checking this book, it was understood that many accounts of the same events would vary to some degree. Nowhere was this truer or more blatant than when our writer's path crossed with that of Luke Spencer's younger sister, Bobbie. The two women often have wildly different recollections of how certain proceedings developed. But in the case of the carbonic snow incident, Bobbie and Lucy are in agreement.

[25] Lucy's note: I guess a cubic zirconia wasn't good enough for them?

[26] Says Luke S, "But lovable."

[27] Aka Elsie Mae Crumholtz. As "Tiffany Hill," Elsie Mae starred in such B movies as *Final Revenge of the Fifty Foot Woman*, *She-Bear Vs. Santa Claus*, and *Mother Blood, Sister Scream*.

Victor, was so strapping and virile. Catch their eye in the moonlight and a woman was in danger of spontaneously ovulating! The head of the clan, Mikkos, was a little out of my age range, but even he had his sex appeal. Too bad they were all a few pickles short of a barrel."

Luke, Laura, and Robert stowed away on Mikkos's yacht, the *Titan*, as the Cassadines and their entourage set sail for a secret facility on their private island off the coast of Venezuela. While traipsing around in the jungle, they learned that Mikkos had developed another use for James and Alexandria's formula.

"Weather control!" barks Luke. Something in the tone of his voice makes me wonder if Tracy has fitted him with a shock collar. I suggest he restock his supply of space cakes, but he doesn't seem to hear me. "The old coot had built a machine straight out of James Bond, aimed it at Port Charles, and turned the dial up to 'Big Chill.' Then the damnedest thing happened: it worked!"

Laura's mother, Dr. Lesley Webber of General Hospital, remembers it clearly. "The city was in great peril. No one was prepared for the cold. People were falling ill in droves, the city's infrastructure was breaking down, and the hospital was operating above capacity. Fuel was running low, the power supply was intermittent, and communications spotty. My husband, Rick, was in the room with GH's chief of staff, Steve Hardy, when the head of the WSB, Ted Ballantine, received Mikkos's ultimatum. Rick later told me[28] Mikkos said he'd make an example of Port Charles; threatened to rain the same terror down on other cities—unless the governments of the world acknowledged him as their supreme leader!"

I would've demanded Prada for life, but that's just me.

"He came dangerously close to destroying Port Charles," Laura[29] tells me over a cup of Corinthos coffee.[30] "Robert and I had managed to get the upper hand on the Cassadine henchmen, but Luke was locked in the control room with Mikkos.

"That fatuous, bloviating throwback had it in his head he wasn't really out to hurt

. . . establish a worldwide
utopia where everyone
lived together in peace!

---

[28] Says Robert S, "In a complete breach of protocol, I might add. Ah, but what're you gonna do? It was the 1980s! You went with your gut, did what felt right. Hell, my digs came equipped with a secret room from which I eavesdropped on loads of people. I can't blame those poor bastards for their loose lips; it was high summer and they were in a deep freeze.

[29] Lucy's note: Laura is presently married to my ex-husband, but I don't hold it against her. She's so beloved around town that disliking Laura is bad for business.

[30] Says Sonny C, "Just ninety-nine cents with the purchase of a muffin at any Perks location!

anyone, was actually only trying to bring the planet into harmony, destroy borders, upend governments, and establish a worldwide utopia where everyone lived together in peace! What a crock. Really he was just your common crook, an extortionist waving a Dr. Evil–sized stick. I put him in his place, cracked the code to his weather machine, and saved the world, easy peasy, lemon squeezy."

With the Cassadines brought to justice and their doomsday doohickey rendered kaput, the atmosphere in Port Charles cleared. Temperatures quickly returned to a status more befitting summer months, the snow melted, and the ordeal was over. Or was it?

"I imagine we've yet to learn the true extent of the Cassadines' villainy," Scorpio contends. "When snow melts, it becomes water. It seeps into the soil, flows into the watershed, replenishes the reservoirs, the river, the lake. We drink it. We bathe in it. We think nothing of it. What about *carbonic* snow? Has anyone conducted any long-term

testing of Port Charles's water sources or its population to determine what side effects there may be to coming into contact with that blight?"[31]

Some scientists and medical professionals dismiss the event as a hoax.

"The Ice Princess 'incident' bears all the hallmarks of a shared social delusion," writes psychiatrist Kevin Collins,[32] "or mass hallucination. Which scenario is more likely? A madman constructed and unleashed a weather machine that rained chemical snow down on the city of Port Charles? Or that it suffered an unusual, unseasonable weather event? Here is the truth: what happened in Port Charles was an early warning of the coming upheaval to our planet's weather patterns; but the citizens of Port Charles

didn't know anything about global warming back then and thus collectively conjured up an explanation that, ludicrous though it was, made sense to them."

Debonair terrorist Jerry Jacks tends to agree. I ran into him over a baccarat table in Monte Carlo. "My dear, delectable Lucy, I have spent the better part of my life seeking the perfect means to wring a great deal of money from a great deal of people who possess great big bank accounts. If a weapon such as purported to have once been wielded by the Cassadines were indeed in existence, I would long ago have acquired it and turned it to my own advantage." I walked away from that table with a shiver, and it wasn't from my backless gown.

Jerry does have a point, Dear Reader. If Luke and Laura and Robert and Tiffany are to be believed, then isn't it likely someone, somewhere, would've made use of Mikkos's machine and James Duvall and Alexandria Quartermaine's secret formula? Or did the WSB confiscate all of the Ice Princess-related materials? Maybe it's all boxed up and gathering dust in some vast government warehouse alongside the Ark of the Covenant. Or . . . is it possible that that formula fell into someone else's hands? One thing we know for sure—the Cassadines are a fertile clan. And they are known to breed.

Either way, not a single flake

of carbonic snow has fallen in the nearly forty years since, and nobody I know has been diagnosed with some horrible carbonic condition, either. So we can safely set aside concerns about a repeat of a blizzard quite that bad, man-made or not.

Earthquakes, on the other hand. . . .

When I say "fault line," you might think "California," "Charlton Heston," or "Have I run out of CoeCoe Cosmetics[33] eye cream?"

> *. . . most residents were unaware of the danger right beneath their feet*

Western New York is not an area one naturally associates with seismic upheaval. But the unlikely truth is Port Charles sits at a very precarious if generally tranquil convergence of tectonic plates. Until 1991, most residents were unaware of the danger right beneath their feet. We were in for a rude awakening.

Tracy Quartermaine was a grown woman living at home with her parents at the time. "Poor Mother and Daddy's beautiful home was destroyed![34] The renovations went on ad infinitum thanks to Monica's subpar contractor, and I was shaking dust from my hair for months!"[35]

That was hardly the worst of it. Not-so-saintly nurse Bobbie Spencer's town house in the historic Brownstone District was practically flattened. One of her tenants—my dear friend Felicia[36]—took a header off the staircase when the railing gave way. She was

---

[33] Sadly no longer for sale. My old company CoeCoe has gone the way of the dodo.

[34] Says Monica Q, "It's MY house, Tracy, your brother gave it to ME."

[35] Again from Monica Q: "It was your mother's contractor, not mine, and you were happy to freeload in my house in spite of the terrible inconvenience to your beauty regimen. In the future, though, you're quite welcome to bed down in the doghouse. I'll even supply you with a flea collar!

[36] An Aztec princess turned private investigator turned memoirist turned mayoral candidate turned interior designer and all-around delight.

even carrying her newborn daughter, Maxie, at the time!

"I burst into the house right after it happened," remembers Felicia's then-husband, my former brother-in-law, the always charming, ever youthful Frisco Jones.[37] "The place was a wreck. Debris everywhere. I called out for Felicia, but there was no answer. Just the sound of Maxie crying. Then I spotted her under a pile of plaster, swaddled in a little pink blanket,[38] wrapped up in Felicia's arms. Somehow Felicia had managed to protect Maxie even as she fell. I don't know why I'm amazed. Felicia's always been my hero.[39]

Felicia suffered pretty bad injuries to her spinal cord—so bad that there was real fear of paralysis. In a regular old city with regular old medical facilities, her chances of ever walking again would've been nil. But as you may already be discovering, Port Charles is not your regular old city; nor are its medical facilities.

The ill and ailing travel here from far and wide in search of healing at our General Hospital.[40] Felicia was delivered into the capable hands of Frisco's brother, my ex-husband,[41] the gone-too-soon neurosurgeon Tony Jones. Tony and the crack team at GH stabilized Felicia and prepped her for a daring surgery to restore her to

The ill and ailing travel here from far and wide in search of healing at our General Hospital

full strength. But it turned out not to be necessary! Frisco crawled into her hospital bed to keep her company in the run-up to surgery—and that was all Felicia needed!

His mere presence has a way of getting one's juices flowing, if you know what I mean, and lo and behold, "The Lady of His Heart"[42] was soon up and at 'em once more . . . although forced to wear a truly unfortunate neck brace for so long, that I began to think it was a practical joke. Those things are a crime against fashion. Someone really should develop a line of designer neck braces. You could have a jazzy one for formal occasions, something in a floral pattern for your everyday garden party, and maybe dress one up with a boa for a twirl on the dance floor. Sounds like a no-brainer, right?

I would've skated right by the 1991 earthquake because, I mean, really—western New York! And it had never happened before in recorded history. Why get you all worried about nothing? What were the chances we'd ever see another one?

Pretty good, as it turned out. A second quake tore through Port Charles in late February of 2018—and this one was even worse.

The vibrant Charles Street neighborhood was the unlucky[43/44]

---

[37] A boy band lead singer turned police officer turned WSB agent.

[38] Says Maxie J, "Pink is still my color."

[39] Says Mac S, "She's *my* hero now, buddy. So back off."

[40] Keep reading! Much more to come on General Hospital, or "GH" to those in the know.

[41] Editor's note: One of at least five!

[42] Says Frisco, "Just one of my number-one singles. Currently available on my album, *WSBe Mine—the Best of Frisco Jones.* Released by L&B Records."

[43] Says current mayor Ned Quartermaine, "It's true that Charles Street has faced more than its fair share of adversity over the years. But that community is not characterized by submission to circumstances—it is instead known for its ability to rise to the occasion.

[44] Editor's note: It has been rumored that Lucy was involved in that.

epicenter of this particular disaster. The stage was set for tumult when the corrupt Mayor Janice Lomax was drummed out of office for rigging her previous election.[45] Ned Quartermaine was running to replace her on a platform promising to draw investment into areas held back by so-called "sluggish" growth—areas like Charles Street.

Ned had the name, the gravitas, the campaign cash, and the support of all the fat cats (not to mention the big-business types). But even with all that going for him, he still couldn't lock up the election. Ned was about to be taught a lesson that the Frank Smiths and Cassadines of the world had learned the hard way: there's just no competing with Port Charles's darling, champion of Charles Street, Laura Collins!

Laura was truly out from under her ex-husband's[46] shadow now, running for mayor on a mission to give the rat bastards hell! "Ned insisted he was only out to improve the lives of my friends and neighbors on Charles Street; but I'd heard Quartermaine promises before."[47] Laura was mopping the floor with Ned, and the ballot measure seeking permission to rezone and redevelop Charles Street was on the rocks, destined for the dustbin of history! Until . . .

"I'd always heard Chamonix's off-piste was off the chart," says Laura's grandson, the precocious and private-schooled Spencer Cassadine. We're having this conversation over Skype from his dorm room in France.

"No one told me you'd have to be off your rocker to try it." At the time of this writing, he's still on crutches, having broken both his legs attempting to land a quadruple Rudy with a tuck and twist off a particularly arduous Alp.

"Spencer's accident happened smack in the middle of the race. I had no choice but to pull out," Laura sighs. "My grandson needed me."[48]

Ned might finally have had the election in the bag—until his ex stepped in to take up Laura's cause! Alexis Davis, attorney-at-law, seemed to be the perfect antidote to Ned's upper-crust, silver spoon candidacy; Alexis is a self-made woman,[49] a legal eagle[50] with a brain that won't quit[51] and a heart that bleeds red, white, and screw-you Big Money! With a bevy of young volunteers at her back, she seemed a shoe-in for victory.

And then the press got hold of the salacious insinuation that she helped Julian Jerome beat the rap on a slew of much-deserved criminal charges. And that was that for Alexis's shot at becoming Port Charles's mayor. Ned won the office, Measure A passed, and real estate developer Jim Harvey commenced his Charles Street construction project posthaste—precipitating our second great earthquake.

Across Port Charles, buildings fell. The dear and dilapidated dive bar The Floating Rib was demolished. The Quartermaine mansion was mincemeat once

---

[45] Lucy's note: This isn't about me!

[46] In the aftermath of the Ice Princess Caper (or delusion), Luke enjoyed a brief, ballyhooed stint as mayor of Port Charles.

[47] In 1994, Laura teamed up with Charles Street pillars the Ward family to battle an ELQ initiative to erect a toxic waste incinerator in their residential neighborhood. For more, see our walking tour, "A Charles Street Stroll."

[48] Lucy's note: I dare say the staff at Spencer's school needed Laura more. Even on his best days that little upstart is a tad, er, formidable.

[49] Editor's note: Self-made in so much as she is the daughter of a famous opera singer and mega-rich madman, Mikkos Cassadine.

[50] Editor's note: Who was disbarred, faked dissociative identity disorder, and infiltrated the Quartermaine household by posing as a butler in order to see her daughter, having previously lost custody on account of murdering a crime boss.

[51] Says Sam M, "Although her judgment in men is pretty suspect."

more. "This time I'll hire my own contractor," Monica vowed. Charles Street was in ruins. Seismologists couldn't understand how a quake of this magnitude had taken place so soon[52] after the last. Suspicion that this was not your usual earthquake was confirmed when a large deposit of natural gas was discovered deep beneath Port Charles. Jim Harvey never had any intention of remaking Charles Street. He was out to grab the land, to tear it up to mine the gas and make a mint!

Now the question on everyone's lips was what did Mayor Quartermaine know, and when did he know it? "I am completely innocent," Ned told me with a straight face. "I knew absolutely nothing about Harvey's plans." I wanted to see the receipts, but the matter of Ned's complicity was soon overshadowed by the fate of Jim Harvey. He'd made a lot of enemies since he blew into town—and wouldn't live long enough to see his plans through to fruition.

With Harvey out of the picture, Port Charles was left to pick up the pieces; so we all got out our brooms and dustpans. Ned, with the help of his wife, that first lady of fusilli Olivia Falconeri, rallied the community and together we rebuilt our city even bigger and better—and more earthquake-proof—than ever before!

The upshot, Dear Reader, is that you're in pretty good shape when you ring up natural disasters and learn that two out of our three were actually man-made. The lesson here is that it isn't the weather you have to watch out for in Port Charles . . . it's the men behind the curtain who make the weather. So don't let the fear of the occasional cataclysm keep you away. We have a lot to offer throughout the year, each season presenting visitors with a bevy of events and celebrations to choose from.

The first big event of the spring occurs when it still feels like winter.[53] Late March is not the most intuitive time to drop in on western New York, but you'd do well to make your travel

[52] Says earth scientist Dr. Melvin Seymour, "Everything is relative."
[53] Says Puerto Rican and onetime PC'er, full-time pop idol Miguel Morez, "Every day in Port Charles feels like winter to me."

plans long in advance. Come the last week of the month there is not a hotel room to be had because that's when throngs of cosmologists, conspiracy theorists, and everyday kooks descend on Port Charles for the "Lumina Look," a yearly hunt for exotic crystals known to pop up on the shores of our fair city. Close readers may recall that the word *Lumina* was found carved into explorer Gaspard Charles's dinghy way back when Port Charles was but a twinkle in his wife Marie's eye. I asked WSB shrink and amateur archaeologist Andre Maddox for his thoughts on our very own convention of crazies.

"I do my best to attend the Lumina Look every year," he says. "For three days an eclectic

reminds me of my ex, Dr. Kevin Collins. Both are psychiatrists, both are brainy, and both are a tad on the sleepy side—that is until you get them talking about something geeky. The intersection of outer space and outlandish opinion really revs Andre's engine: "The Goldilocks zone is also known as the habitable zone. It's that area of space surrounding a star that's neither too hot nor too cold to sustain life—or, life as we know it."

Either Andre is talking about a really terrible movie or trying to tell me there are aliens on planet Lumina! And these aliens have something to do with the disappearance of Gaspard Charles all the way back in the seventeenth century!

> *Declassified Pentagon files aside, there's no real evidence that aliens exist . . .*

mix of people from across the country and around the world turn the city upside down in search of Lumina crystals, and at night come together to examine the historical record, present new findings, and trade theories on the ultimate fate of Gaspard Charles and how it may connect to the planet Lumina."

Say what?

"Lumina orbits the nearby star Proxima Centauri. It was discovered by astronomers in the late twentieth century," Maddox adds. "While little is known about Lumina, one key fact makes it worthy of particular notice and continued study: it exists within the Goldilocks zone."

You're telling me it found just the right bed to sleep in?

"In a manner of speaking!" Dr. Maddox

Andre tries to sell me that this is not the case. "Declassified Pentagon files aside, there's no real evidence that aliens exist, certainly not ones hailing from Lumina." Then he casts a quick look around—as if to make sure no one is watching—and leans in close. "But don't you think it's strange that upon his disappearance, Gaspard Charles is thought to have carved the word *Lumina* into his boat, hundreds of years before the planet was discovered? And that crystals thought to be native to Lumina have been found in Port Charles—and nowhere else?"

Yes, Andre, I do think that's strange! Almost as strange as the fact that in an era marked by artificial intelligence, cloned sheep, and cops on Segways, we have yet to solve the problem of visible panty lines. But since there's no annual gathering here devoted to untangling that knot, I bundled up and hauled myself to the Great Lawn in Elmwood Park for the culmination of the Look. That's where I found hundreds of alien aficionados staring up at the night sky—as well as on-again/off-again PCPD police commissioner Anna Devane and her daughter, Dr. Robin Scorpio-Drake.

It isn't the sort of place I'd expect to find two people I know to be so down-to-earth; so I had to ask what brings them to this fraternity of fruitcakes. They steal looks at each other and for a moment I wonder if I'm about to get Anna's patented runaround response. After all, she is a reformed spy and not known for telling the truth.[54] But Robin is about as honorable as they come. "Are you kidding? This is the celestial event of the year. It's the only night Lumina can be glimpsed with the naked eye—and the best place in all the world to do it is here in Port Charles. I look up at Lumina and wonder—"

But here Anna chimes in to finish Robin's sentence. "Maybe someone is looking back at me." Robin puts her arm around her mother's shoulders and leans into her—and suddenly everything is wistful, like they just put their true love on a plane to Lisbon with letter of transit. So I follow their gaze into the sky, and wouldn't you know it, one star in particular glints . . . like a crystal. Or a jewel. The kind that looks best on my ring finger.

If standing on a lakeshore in March sends the wrong kind of shivers down your spine, you could delay your visit to April—but tarry no longer than that! You and yours would be hopping mad not to make your trip to Port Charles in time for the annual Quartermaine family Charity Easter Egg Hunt and Bonnet Bonanza! Our president has nothing on Monica and her grandson, Michael,[55] who together have kept up a decades-old tradition established by the late and much-missed family matriarch, Lila Quartermaine.[56]

The pastels are on parade and PAAS are on point every Easter Sunday when Michael dons his bunny suit, and Monica gussies up the gardens and throws open the gates to Port Charles's younger set. Kiddies pour forth[57] in search of eggs delicately painted with the Quartermaine family crest and depictions of memorable scenes from the family history.[58] Artist-turned-nurse Elizabeth Webber donates her time and skills to the decorating effort. "Eggshell isn't my preferred medium, but between raising three boys and managing patients at General Hospital,[59] it's hard to find time to devote to canvas." Proceeds from the gala go to fund the A. J. Quartermaine Clinic, which provides free and low-cost health care to the underserved in PC's Elm Street neighborhood.[60]

---

[54] Editor's note: Bobbie Spencer, Tracy Quartermaine, Terry Brock, and the corpses of Katherine Bell and Damian Smith all told me to tell you, "HA."

[55] Editor's note: Over the years, Michael's last names have included Morgan, Corinthos, and Quartermaine—depending on who claimed his paternity and/or custody. For the purposes of clarity, and not to run afoul of certain oversensitive and "allegedly" criminal elements, we shall refer to him as Michael Corinthos.

[56] Editor's note: For more on Lila and her famous family, see the section entitled "The Quick and the Quartermaine."

[57] Says Quartermaine heiress Tracy: "And trample the topiary and imperil the prize parterre. I lobbied Mother to nix the Easter apocalypse years ago—and what did I get for it? Banishment!"

[58] Like the time Edward sent daughter Tracy packing for withholding his heart medication when he faked a heart attack; or the time he sent her packing for running over her son Ned Ashton's ex-wife, Jenny. Or the time he sent her packing for making her son's THIRD (but not last) wife, Lois, so miserable that SHE went packing! Collect 'em all! Says Lucy, "Technically there was a 'wife' in between Jenny and Lois named Katherine, but we don't count that blackmailing, gold-digging, wannabe blue-blooded snake."

[59] Says Sam M, "And yet she still finds time to lie, slap, and sleep around."

[60] Says Sonny C, "You're better off seeking medical attention from a mortician. That clinic is as unreliable as its namesake."

Some summer in Provence (how tired!); others in the Hamptons (so bourgeois!). Suckers, the lot of them! Those in the know avoid the hoi polloi and dinner-reservation derby of the more conventional scenes by slipping away to Port Charles instead! Here you can go farm-to-table-to-mouth with ease,[61] and soak up plenty of vitamin D all along the lake. You'll find no dearth of opportunities to see some skin and let your skin be seen at Holt State Park,[62] where the beachier set steal away from Memorial Day on. To join them, cruise north out of downtown on Route 31 and follow the signs all the way to the end of the road. There you'll find ten miles of unspoiled dunes and picture-perfect lake views. Families tend to favor the beaches nearest the parking lots. Take care not to amble too far to the west—unless you don't mind ambling in the buff. Freer spirits who scale the dune half a mile from the main entrance and slide down the other side will find themselves smack in the bosom of the only nude beach in the county; or so I've heard. I only get naked for the Nurses Ball.[63] But I've long heard that this is the place where the va-va-va-Who's-Whom among us go to do battle with tan lines. I won't name names, but if you've ever beheld the Magic Milo[64] striptease, you're sure to behold some familiarly full monty at the nude beach. . . .

For more chaste fare, amble east from the main beach. You'll come across hard bodies, but these ones are clad in wet suits; and they're not sunning themselves on the shore. They're bobbing some distance out from land waiting for the perfect wave.

This is our surf scene! No, that is not a typo! It exists—thanks to the pioneering efforts of my good buddy, Australian[65] expat and surf ambassador Jasper Jacks.[66] Jacks—"Jax" to his friends—cut his teeth raiding corporate coffers and flying the big blue yonder. Jax makes it a point never to stray too far from a beach, no matter how big a deal he's putting together. So when he touched down in Port Charles in 1996,[67]

[61] Says Olivia Falconeri, half-owner of Port Charles's only five-star hotel and restaurant, the Metro Court: "Every week the food director and I take a field trip to the Port Charles Public Market and we stock up on fresh organic produce and meat and flowers and oh, *mamma mia*, the cheese! Until I moved to Port Charles, I thought there were only two places you could get Parmesan this good—the old country and the great beyond! We take our haul back to the hotel and that's what goes into our award-winning meals. For good wholesome food, you can't do better than the Public Market. If you're lucky you might just run into the Quartermaine family's personal chef, Cook Two. Be sure to ask for a tour! Cook Two loves showing off the kitchen!" *The Port Charles Public Market is located in the Asian Quarter at 280 Union Street North. It is open Saturdays from 5:00 a.m.–3:00 p.m. and Tuesdays and Thursdays from 6:00 a.m. –1:00 p.m.*
[62] Naming rights were purchased in 1984 by the frequently shirtless, briefly stinking rich illegitimate son of Edward Quartermaine, Jimmy Lee Holt.
[63] Editor's note: Lucy has a peculiar habit of winding up disrobed onstage while hosting the annual effort to fund the fight against HIV and AIDS. "She claims 'accidental nudity,'" says Bobbie S., "but at this point the ball programs should come with a parental warning." For more about Port Charles's biggest party of the year, please read on.
[64] A seminal Nurses Ball act. Past performers include PCPD pinup Nathan West, man of godly abs Griffin Munro, and the man himself, personal trainer and bodyguard to "legitimate" businessmen, Prince Pectoral himself, Milo Giambetti.
[65] So many Australians have found second homes in Port Charles that it is often referred to as Down Under Up Over. Locals affectionately refer to the 1000 block of North Yale Street as Little Sydney, or "LiSy."
[66] Also not a typo.
[67] Editor's note: Jax was invited to Port Charles by Lois Cerullo—previously referred to as Ned Ashton's third-but-not-last wife—in order to wrest back control of her company, L&B Records, from Ned's meddling grandfather, Edward.

practically the first thing he did[68] was take a trip out to the lake to survey the scene.

"It was bleak," Jax tells me over a long black at Kelly's,[69] the greasiest of spoons and a Port Charles institution (try the BLT[70]—or Ruby's chili[71]—or the bacon, egg, and cheese on Kaiser—or the short stack—or the . . . well, you get the drift).[72] "There wasn't a board in sight. No surf station. No weather monitor. No juice bar! How can you surf without a ginger-mango-kale under your belt?" How indeed?

"The beach at Holt State Park did have one thing going for it, though," Jax notes. "Waves! Waves for days! I'm not talking about your piddling, inland sea ankle busters,[73] either. You could take off on a bomb[74] and ride it all the way to Toronto! Lois had told me the water was not to be missed, but I thought she was taking the mickey out of me. What does a western New Yorker by way of Brooklyn know about surfing? My hair was sure to have better waves! But boy was I wrong. I've never had a better ride than in Port Charles."

Suddenly Jax's eyes mist and I get the feeling he's not just referring to the water. Is there anything sexier than a man who isn't afraid to cry? I give him a moment to throttle

[68] After attempting to romance Lois away from Ned; after making enemies out of a slew of Quartermaines; after falling head over heels for pint-sized supermodel Brenda Barrett . . .

[69] We passed a s cafe on our stroll to Kelly's, but Jax refused to even take a whiff of Corinthos coffee. "I could make better coffee with tea leaves."

[70] Says Heather W, "They do something to the bacon. I can't put my finger on it. But whatever it is, it drives my taste buds CRAZY."

[71] But be careful. It has a way of whupping your butt, just like its namesake—onetime madam, sometime busybody, and all-time heart of gold, Ruby Anderson.

[72] Kelly's Diner & Boarding House is located at 324 Wharf Street. Call (716) 555-BLTS for today's specials!

[73] Waves too small to ride.

[74] An uncommonly big wave—all too common in Port Charles.

his emotion and me a moment to throttle my appetite, and I wonder to myself—why did I never get together with this handsome, heartfelt hunk? Then I remember it's because his heart was spoken for the moment he laid eyes on my muse, the Face of Deception Cosmetics, Brenda Barrett.[75]

I ask him if he's heard from her lately. He responds by avoiding my eyes in favor of the menu and gripes about the fact that Bobbie[76] still hasn't gotten around to getting Kelly's a liquor license. It's clear Jax doesn't want to talk about Brenda,[77] but not reckoning with her would leave any guide to Port Charles vastly incomplete. For such a short supermodel, she sure casts a long shadow. Bratty Brenda started out life in Port Charles as the ward to her older half sister, my former colleague, mover and shaker Julia Barrett. Julia was ill-equipped to handle Brenda,[78] who spent her high school years honing her skills for mischief in one long failed campaign to keep the sweet, innocent Karen Wexler from uniting with smolder-y stud muffin John "Jagger"[79] Cates.

Brenda couldn't turn Jagger's head for long, but he was the exception to her allure, not the rule. Not that it would matter. Jagger became "Jagger-Wha?" the moment she locked eyes with Sonny Corinthos. Back then Brenda was still just a teenager,[80] and Sonny a humble small businessman.[81] But their courtship set Port Charles on fire![82] I'd look at them look at each other and suddenly feel a hankering for a cigarette—and I never smoked a day in my life.

Alas, Brenda proved too willful for Sonny. Since I've known him, he's always been attracted to headstrong women—but there's only so much stubbornness a proud[83] man can take before he expects his lady to yield.[84] The story goes like this: Word had gotten around that maybe not all of Sonny's business interests were what one might call "legitimate."[85] In order to prove her nay-saying friends wrong, Brenda wired up and attempted to coax bona fide proof directly from her man's mouth. But Sonny was onto Brenda. The woman who would become his first wife, Lily Rivera, sniffed out her scheme and tattled. Sonny dropped Brenda

[75] Editor's note: When listening to Lucy's interview recordings, I mistook "Brenda" for "Brender"; such is the strength of Jax's Australian accent.

[76] Ruby died in 1999, leaving Kelly's to Bobbie Spencer and her brother, Luke, whom Ruby had looked after since they were kids. "It's a bit of a stretch to say Ruby 'looked after' Bobbie," says Lucy. "Unless facilitating Bobbie's first career as a teenaged hooker qualifies."

[77] Says Skye C-Q, "No, just obsess over her."

[78] Says Carly C: "Be fair to Julia. You'd need a leash and a shock collar to handle Brenda."

[79] Editor's note: Apparently the name "Jagger" is derived from a West Yorkshire dialect. It means "peddler." What John "Jagger" Cates peddled is a mystery. Lucy's note: He wasn't "peddling" so much as pedaling—away, that is, from all the ladies grasping for a piece of his underwear-model body. Hubba-hubba!

[80] But legal!

[81] Says Mac S, "If you can call running The Paradise Lounge strip club 'humble' and hooking his dancers on drugs a 'business.'"

[82] Editor's note: Literally. People died, including but not limited to the woman Sonny is said to have consoled himself with after one bad breakup with Brenda, Lily Rivera.

[83] Says Alexis D, "Proud? Try pigheaded, sexist, or self-absorbed."

[84] Says Lois C, "You want to know the truth about Sonny? Take it from someone who knew him growing up in the old neighborhood. Sonny likes to come off all "Big Boss Man," sharkskin suit and pinkie ring, rolling out the lucci like. But he's a mama's boy at heart. A little flash will always catch his eye, but really all he yearns for is the knowledge that every night he'll come home to a healthy dose of adulation from his yes-woman. Brenda could never be that. Carly Benson, on the other hand . . ."

[85] Says Ava J, "Are you telling me he's not merely a modest coffee importer? Say it ain't so!"

like a bad cannoli. For a time, Brenda took comfort with GH orderly/Outback[86] bartender, Miguel Morez.[87] Later her friend and business partner, Lois, introduced Brenda to Jax, with whom she plotted to make Sonny jealous. It worked—but not before Brenda fell for Jax for real!

"Brenda got hit by a car outside Luke's,"[88] Jax reminds me. "The recovery was hard; and harder still with that mook[89] hovering around. She needed a break, needed to get out of Port Charles. So I had the jet[90] gassed up and flew us both out to Malibu."

"I remember it well," says Brenda. I ran into her in Paris, where she lent her celebrity to a charity gala benefitting the Alliance to Save Exploited Children. Her entourage taps their feet. They may as well not exist. Heck, me either! Brenda is alone with her memories. "He treated me to California cuisine, a Rodeo Drive shopping spree . . . and the sight of him emerging from the ocean in a Speedo. He was a Greek myth given form."

"She has a habit for hyperbole," Jax tells me back in Port Charles. But he's blushing. I didn't think Jax had it in him to blush.

Brenda goes on. "He was an Adonis, and I said so to his face.

But as impressive though his physique may be, it's nothing compared to his soul. He's as lovely a human being as I've ever known, put up with all of my schemes and shenanigans, even agreed to one of my less-inspired plots. I thought that by spending time with Jax I'd make Sonny jealous. What I didn't count on was how I'd feel after Jax kissed me in Malibu."

"Our first proper kiss," says Jax. He almost sounds like he's mourning.

Brenda tells me they landed in Malibu as friends. "But we returned to Port Charles as something more. I did my best to ignore it and recommit to winning Sonny back."

And so she did. Everything might have worked out for Sonny and Brenda—if Sonny's then-wife, Lily (the one who torpedoed Sonny and Brenda in the first place), hadn't wound

[86] The Outback Bar & Club (5563 King Place) was located at the corner of North Yale in, you guessed it, LiSy. It was run by Mac Scorpio and hosted memorable performances from Connor Olivera, Alan "Karaoke" Quartermaine, Eddie Maine and the Idle Rich, and Miguel Morez. The Outback has since closed down and been replaced by a poke-bowl restaurant.

[87] Editor's note: Yes, Miguel Morez of international pop stardom. Before hitting the big-time Miguel—a look-alike for Menudo star Ricky Martin if ever there was—spent a few years in Port Charles pulling children from car wrecks, hosing down GH bedpans, and slinging piña coladas and Felicia Flips at the Outback.

[88] Editor's note: An eponymously named blues club housed in the space formerly occupied by the strip bar, The Paradise Lounge. The club has since closed down. The Ava Jerome Gallery stands in its place.

[89] Editor's note: He means Sonny.

[90] Says Lucy, "One of two, I've heard. There's also a yacht, The *Isabella*, a vineyard in Coonawarra, a villa in Cap d'Antibes, and probably a moon base, to boot."

up pregnant. Though Sonny loved Brenda, he would not abandon his wife just as she was about to make him a father. Brenda went running to Jax and they were soon wed on his yacht, the *Isabella*, clinking champagne glasses—just as a very loud boom was echoing across Port Charles. Sonny and his wife, Lily, had announced their pregnancy to a club full of friends and family. As the evening drew to a close, Sonny found himself too drunk to drive, so Lily went to pull the car around—only to perish in a bomb believed meant for Sonny.[91] The Corinthos marriage was cruelly snuffed out . . . just as Jax and Brenda's was beginning.

"Our honeymoon took us from the Mediterranean all the way to Alaska,[92] where I introduced Brenda to my parents.[93] If I'd known then what I know now, I'd have scuttled the ship and convinced Brenda to make a home with me right there in the woods. But Brenda had her heart set on returning to Port Charles. And for me, home was wherever Brenda was. So back we went . . . right into the storm of Sonny's grief. Sonny got over Lily's[94] loss—quicker than you might think—and put himself right back in Brenda's path. One thing led to another,[95]

and . . . well, it wasn't meant to be. Over the years we had another go or two, but we could never make it work."[96]

In Paris, Brenda asks me about Jax. I hear the sad, wistful tinkle of a piano. I look around but see no ivory anywhere in sight. Am I imagining things? Or does Brenda carry a soundtrack with her wherever she goes? "It's been a while since he and I have spoken," she says. "Things didn't end well the last time we saw each other.[97] How is he?"[98]

I hesitate, but not so long that she questions my response. "Really, really well." My lie seems to satisfy her . . . if not give her peace.

Back in Port Charles, what was supposed to be just coffee has evolved into Jax's third slice of pie. Talk of Brenda seems to require loads of fuel. Does he have any regrets, I wonder? His gaze falls on the dessert case and lingers there a moment. But rather than signal the waitress, he pushes his plate of crumbs toward the center of the table. "Phil Edwards once said that the best surfer out there is the one having the most fun. I had

---

[91] "My client is a law-abiding citizen," says Sonny's lawyer, Diane Miller, "whom some underworld elements occasionally mistake for a competitor." "Or pushover," adds Sonny with a growl.

[92] Lucy's note: Not my idea of a honeymoon.

[93] Lucy's note: Definitely not my idea of a honeymoon.

[94] Says Luke S, "It might have helped dull his grief that he got to personally deliver news of his survival to the man who set the bomb—his own father-in-law, Hernando. Talk about a cold son of a bitch. Almost as cold as Sonny. I hear he visited ol' 'nando in his sickbed and left him with a way out." Lily's father, reputed mob boss Hernan Rivera, is said to have distrusted Sonny to the point of wanting him dead. Unfortunately for all involved, the bomb Hernando set for Sonny claimed the lives of his own daughter and unborn grandchild instead.

[95] Editor's note: *One thing* being the return of Jax's first wife, the presumed dead Miranda; *another thing* being Sonny and Brenda trysting while trapped in a cave-in.

[96] Says Sonny C, "The problem with golden boy is he has too much regard for himself. If his parents hadn't blown up his ego, he'd know better than to go chasing after women who have anything to do with yours truly. Brenda, Carly, Sam—they all know what Jax doesn't. He just doesn't measure up."

[97] Lucy's note: I remember it well. Picture it: Nurses Ball, 2013. Port Charles has pulled out the stops and pulled together once more to raise money to fund the fight against HIV/AIDS. Brenda has returned for the party with her fiancé—Jax! But it isn't long before she's sneaking out to visit Sonny . . . and wonder if there's a chance they might reunite! So much for Jax and Brenda's latest triumphant reunion.

[98] Says Carly C, "Translation: Does he talk about me? Does he miss me? Will he take me back?"

the most fun with Brenda. But believe it or not I'm managing to have plenty of fun without her." I wonder if he's putting me on. But I've known Jax a long time. He's fabulous, but no fabulist. "My life is full. I have my daughter,[99] my work, and my board. The only thing I'm missing is something I'm never missing for long. I find it in the water."

Happiness is a long hollow,[100] Jax says. "Surf has always been restorative for me. The joy of the ride crowds out all the worries, all the bad feelings you carry with you into the water. By the time I'm ready to pack it in, I've forgotten what sent me scrambling to escape in the first place. I'm back to full hearts and ready to face the world again. That's why I was so mystified by the absence of a Port Charles surf culture. No one seemed to have any idea the kind of release that awaited them, just minutes outside the city." It was after a particularly bad blowup with Brenda—and a particularly epic surf session—that Jax urgently sought something else to concentrate on. "And that's how the Triple J Surf School[101] and the annual Great Waves of the Great Lakes Surf Rally were born." Now in its twentieth year, the rally

[99] Lucy's note: Jax has a lovely daughter, Josslyn, with Carly Corinthos. She was married to Jax for a time—between marriages to Sonny, of course.
[100] The hollow section of a great wave; like riding in a tunnel.
[101] Call 716-555-WAVE to book private lessons or inquire about camps. All dillas, grommets, hodads, and kooks welcome!

attracts spectators from all over the world to Port Charles, where they thrill to the exploits of the surf world's premiere competitors, participate in technique intensives, and gamely try to snag a surfer of their own for private lessons. Adonises abound!

If the thought of such physical exertion has been the source of so much corruption. This event is the exception." The event is sponsored by ELQ International, but there was a time the Quartermaines didn't want to go near anything involving boats and/or sea— and I'm not talking about the SS *Tracy*[102] or its namesake.

. . . hot guy + boat = hell yes!

does not comport with your concept of summer, take in the Classic Charles Regatta. For Corinthos family counsel Diane Miller, the event "Makes me feel like I've stepped into some F. Scott Fitzgerald novel." Most folks in their crisp polos, straw boaters, and designer summer frocks straight from the pages of *Crimson Magazine* tend to agree. The regatta is a unique event with its own distinctive blend of racing and waterfront parties. Calling at three of the finest docks in Port Charles, it brings together a collection of yachts and their crews to share and celebrate the art of sailing.

Jax—who before recent revitalization efforts long bemoaned the city's general neglect of the urban waterfront—took me aside to exclaim, "For so long, the waterfront

Former Port Charles resident and now FBI agent Jagger Cates wrote me an email from his home in San Francisco to give me the full scoop on the mishap that has become a local nautical cautionary tale. "It all started when Jason asked Karen to join him for a ride on the Quartermaine boat.[103] I told Karen I didn't think it was a good idea, not just because she gets seasick, but because I didn't want her in an enclosed space with anyone but me!" Karen totally went anyway, because hot guy+boat = hell yes! Jason's attempts to pilot his own "Love Boat" went the way of Gilligan's Island when the engine gave out again, leaving him and Karen[104] powerless in the face of Mother Nature's wrath. While a hormonal storm brewed between the two

[102] Editor's note: In 1991, the Quartermaine family had again fallen on hard times. Ned had arranged for a shipment of machinery that would boost productivity at their ailing cannery. The machinery was due to arrive on a cargo ship: the S.S. *Tracy*. Also on board were dangerous chemicals. An area environmental group, the Greenbelts, came out in force to protest the *Tracy*'s presence. Upon arrival—but before the ship could dock and off-load its company-saving machinery—the ship exploded and sunk! Sabotage was suspected, and the leader of the Greenbelts, Spencer's cousin Jenny Eckert, was arrested for the crime, as was the police commissioner's younger brother, Mac! It would be some time before the full truth about the *Tracy*'s sinking was revealed. Read on for our entry on the Founder's Day holiday for more.

[103] Says Monica Q, "This was a few years prior to the accident that reshaped Jason. He was still a teenager then. He and his girlfriend Karen Wexler couldn't get enough of each other."

[104] Lucy's note: Unbeknownst to Jason and Karen, Jagger had tagged along. He'd been working on the engine belowdecks when Jason started it up. Jagger hit his head and fell unconscious while Jason took Karen on their joyride.

boys over Karen, the maiden in question knew from the heavy rain and strong winds there was more at risk than having to pick a winner and a loser. From what Jagger told me,[105] he tried to fix the engine while Karen attempted to get a weather report on the radio. When a huge wave hit the boat, Jagger was washed overboard. "I thought it was over for me, but then Karen[106] pulled me back in."

After being thrown from the ship, the threesome found themselves washed up on a desert island.[107] "Add a coconut tree and unlimited rum and you have my biggest fantasy," exclaimed Diane Miller when I told her the story. "When we all discovered we were on the island, I thought it was going to be brief," Jagger recounts. "Of course Mommy and Daddy Quartermaine were going to send out the National Guard to find their little prince." Jagger was shocked to discover that they didn't tell anybody that they were going out on the boat.

A search was nevertheless underway— not only for the kids, but also two escaped convicts, brothers Cal and Joseph Atkins. They too were on the island, but more by choice than by accident. Though hiding from the law, Cal and Joseph managed to keep breaking it, attacking Karen. "I worked through my fear of heights to climb to the top of a cliff where Cal was holding Karen." Three went up, three went down—but with only two of them alive. Jason arrived at the bottom of the cliff just in time to see Cal plummet to his death. Jason's

brother A.J. and father, Alan, located the kids and sailed them home to safety. Jason, Jagger, and Karen made a pact never to speak of what happened on the island.[108] The danger was seemingly over, until Joseph reappeared to blackmail the kids for the role they played in his brother's death. Suspecting the kids were up to something, Police Commissioner Sean Donely had them watched and followed to the site where they agreed to meet and pay off Joseph. But he wasn't alone; Cal was with him. He'd survived his fall,[109] but his days of escape were over. Cal was apprehended, and Joseph was as well soon after. Jagger and Karen had a lot of tumult[110] ahead of them, but they eventually were wed and left town. Jason stayed—but he wasn't the same Jason for long.

The point, people, is this: don't skimp on boat safety!

Port Charles doesn't slow down or slouch in autumn, either. Be it a foliage tour or an apple-picking expedition to Beecher's Corners, you're sure to get your fill of fall fun. Start celebrating with a visit to the annual Port Charles Harvest Hoedown Weekend! The hoedown takes place in Elm Park every Columbus Day weekend. With so many activities to choose from, everyone in your family is guaranteed to find something to suit their fancy. Let Quartermaine family chef Cook Two teach you how to make your own cider, then grab some allergy medicine and try the hay bale climb, or even take a ride on llamas

---

[105] Lucy's note: I had to read between the lines a bit, because Jagger's account had Jason "weeping in fear in the corner, like an itty-bitty baby."

[106] Editor's note: Karen has since died and Jason's accident has robbed him of his memory of this incident. We only have Jagger's account of the events.

[107] Spoon Island isn't the only one.

[108] Lucy's note: Pacts like this never work out for long in Port Charles.

[109] Editor's note: Such survivals are surprisingly commonplace in Port Charles. Read on for many more tales of life beyond death.

[110] Says Robin S, "There's no getting around this one: all of Jagger and Karen's problems started with Sonny Corinthos. I would later grow to care very much about him, but when I first knew Sonny, he was slime. He got Karen hooked on drugs and put her up to strip in his club, The Paradise Lounge. Later he took control of Jagger's boxing contract and supposedly ordered him to take a fall, which Jagger naturally declined to do. It's possible Sonny even tried to have Jagger killed. Sonny has come a long way, but I have to be careful that I never forget where he started.

on loan from the PC Zoo! Other happenings include antique farm-tool demonstrations given by Jason Morgan; farm-animal meet 'n' greets; and live music, courtesy of Eddie Maine and the Idle Rich! For the little ones, we'll have storytelling with Curtis Ashford, face painting by Franco Baldwin, and a crafting booth in which kids help Elizabeth Webber make paper toys for the residents of the Shady Brook Sanitarium.

This year we're also very excited to welcome the New York Colonial Regiment Militia Re-enactors! Members of the regiment, led by Revolutionary War aficionados Max and Milo Giambetti, will be on the soccer field all weekend giving time-period specific demonstrations. Attendees are welcome to take part in marching drills, watch a musket demo, and finding out more about life as a member of the Colonial militia, which was encamped in Port Charles in 1776.

Be sure to come hungry and feast on delicious fare, courtesy of a parade of food trucks headlined by Pozzulo's Fine Italian

Eatery and Noodle Buddha. Be sure to cast your vote in the yearly scarecrow contest. Last year's winner, infectious disease specialist[111] Dr. Hamilton Finn, will be on hand as a guest judge. Apples for our popular slingshot at the Connie Falconeri Memorial Koi Pond are available for purchase through the hoedown.

More adult fare is being offered should the hoedown feel like too much family for you there. Any Port Charles University student will tell you that Port Charles in the fall means just one thing to them: Oktoberfest! This waterfront-situated event is held every year on the first Thursday and Friday of the month. In addition to eating, drinking, and dancing, visitors can enjoy a colorful parade led by the marching band from PCU.

Oktoberfest has become a huge draw, so accommodations and transportation should be booked well in advance if you plan on attending. Here's a quick tutorial on how the Port Charles Oktoberfest[112] started, what it entails, and how to best plan your visit.

HOW DID PORT CHARLES END UP WITH THE FOURTEENTH LARGEST OKTOBERFEST IN NEW YORK STATE?

In the late nineteenth century, Port Charles welcomed a large influx of German immigrants after a train from Ellis Island bound for Minnesota was accidentally misdirected due to illegible handwriting. One of those new residents was Fritz Obrecht.[113] Fritz took one look at the drab, colorless garb worn by the locals and saw an opportunity to liven up their lives and line his pockets. He launched the first Oktoberfest to market his family's famous dirndls.[114] It wasn't long before the locals fell in love with the colorful clothes and endless beer. A new Port Charles tradition was born.

---

[111] *Says* Grins Anna D, "Not to be confused with infections *fun* specialist."

[112] The original Oktoberfest began in Germany 1810. It was held in honor of the wedding of Crown Prince Ludwig of Bavaria and Princess Therese of Saxony-Hildburghausen.

[113] Editor's note: *Extensive Ancestry.com* sessions have determined that Fritz is indeed a distant relation of Swiss doctor Liesl Obrecht, once chief of staff of General Hospital.

[114] Editor's note: A dirndl is a dress worn in Austria, the South Tyrol, and Bavaria. It is based on the traditional clothing of Alps peasants. It is thus no coincidence that the dirndl is a favorite article of attire of Dr. Obrecht.

MUST I DRESS UP IN ORDER TO ATTEND?

Does Sonny Corinthos like coffee? Of course you do, or you might find yourself floating amidst the docks. Lederhosen are required for the men, and dirndl are compulsory for ladies.

Wyndham's Department Store[115] carries a limited supply of both in the weeks leading up to Oktoberfest.

WHAT IS THERE TO EAT?

Here's one of Oktoberfest's number one fans, Michael Corinthos, to give you the dish on what to consume: "Besides primo beer served in those cool, frosted glass mug things,[116] the food tents have grilled sausages up the wazoo, roast chicken, giant pretzels, and—for anyone with a stomach of steel (Hi, Mom!)— wild oxen."

[115] 620 North Main Street
[116] Editor's note: "Steins."

WHAT IS THERE TO DO BESIDES EAT AND DRINK?

While mainly for adults, Oktoberfest does have a little something to keep the kids occupied. Look for carnival rides such as the "Helena Höllenblitz,"[117] or for those seeking something less devilish, the " Krampus Krinoline," a merry-go-round set to nursery rhymes sung in German by our very own Dr. Obrecht.

While Port Charles enjoys all the celebrations typical to the winter season, there is one that is particular to our city—the annual celebration of Port Charles's origins on Founder's Day. Everyone who is anyone (and everyone else to boot) comes out on December 2 to lift high a glass to the woman who started it all: Marie Charles. A parade from the waterfront—where our founders first landed—to the site of their original settlement at City Hall marks the route Marie and her fellow settlers took when they brought Port Charles forth from the wilderness. At night Wyndham's puts on a fireworks show to rival anything Macy's has ever had on offer—and then the parties begin!

Oh, the parties! Everyone gets glammed up and hits a circuit of soirees that crisscross the city, from the Quartermaine estate to the top of the Metro Court. Tradition has it that the city's restaurants are closed the whole next day to allow their employees a day of rest—to say nothing of the citywide hangover.

And to think—the last Founder's Day ever might have taken place in 1991 had a bunch of cretinous criminals gotten their way. It's a complicated tale but luckily for us, Robin Scorpio-Drake happened to be in town one weekend to celebrate her friend Elizabeth Webber's birthday. Between giving Carly Corinthos a hard time and reminding everyone that Jason Morgan is a saint, she found just enough time to share with me a bottle of wine—and the story.

"My mother is a beautiful, able, formidable woman. In my observation, that combination of qualities can inspire a dangerous obsession in some men," Robin tells me. "None more dangerous than the terrorist Cesar Faison.[118] The incident with the Cartel is a perfect example of how Faison's need to possess my mother has had ripple effects on nearly every citizen of Port Charles.

"In 1991, my parents made another of their many attempts at domestic tranquility. They got married again[119] in a lavish ceremony[120] hosted by Lila Quartermaine," continues Robin. "News of their wedding reached Faison, to whom it was catnip. He returned to torture my mother and everyone in her orbit."

Robin takes a deep breath and tells me—and here's where it gets confusing. "So I'll try to boil it down for you. When Faison resurfaced,[121] it was revealed that he had thrown in with

---

[117] Editor's note: Roughly translated from the German as "Helena from Hell."

[118] Editor's note: Faison was once the head of the criminal espionage service known as the DVX, an agency so shadowy that the meaning of its acronym is considered top secret by its opposite, the WSB. Many of the worst acts ever to befall our city can be traced back to Faison in one way or another.

[119] Lucy's note: I remember it well. Perhaps the most beautiful ceremony I've ever had the pleasure of attending.

[120] Says Tracy Q, "You weren't invited! You crashed it!"

[121] Editor's note: Declassified WSB files place Faison's previous appearance in Port Charles the year before, when he took up residence at Wyndemere on Spoon Island and embarked on a quest to collect crystals thought to be native to the planet Lumina, thus giving rise to the first Lumina Look.

a mysterious cabal known simply as the 'Cartel,'" Robin points out. "Eventually, the other members of his group were unmasked: Harlan Barrett,[122] Leopold Taub,[123] and "Lord" Larry Ashton.[124] They'd teamed up to develop a poison gas—carbon disulfide—that they might then sell to the one percent and up. Needing a base from which to manufacture the gas, they hit upon ELQ's cannery[125]—a perfect cover for their operation. They even got Luke Spencer's look-alike, cousin Bill Eckert, to run the whole thing.

"Soon, all of Port Charles's finest spymasters[126] were on the case and attempting to intervene," Robin relates. "In an effort to cut them off at the knees, Faison poisoned Sean's wife, Tiffany,[127] just like he had done to Paul's daughter, Susan. That was Faison's MO—seizing control of people by hurting those they love. At the same time Faison was dropping poison all over Port Charles, he was deploying hypnotism and mind-control techniques to sow confusion and mistrust between my parents and my uncle Mac."

Robin has a sip of her Chardonnay before continuing. "Eventually, the Scoobies—with the help of Bill Eckert—turned the tables on Faison and the Cartel. The bad guys gathered their backs to demonstrate the uses of carbon disulfide—by releasing it upon the unsuspecting citizens of Port Charles," Robin says. "Luckily my parents and Mac got wind of the plan in time to switch out the gas with a harmless fog. My parents burst in on Faison and his crew, putting them under arrest. But Faison wasn't done yet.

"He slithered out of custody and abducted my mom, putting in place a story that she went with him of her own will," Robin recalls. "But as she later told me, Faison soon came to realize that she'd never be happy without one thing: me. So, in a last-ditch attempt to bend Mom to his will Faison sent his own mother, Sybil McTavish, to infiltrate the security team that had been placed around me. Faison's efforts were no match for my dad and Holly Sutton; and in a case of Oedipal rage gone amok, he shot and killed his own mother!"

All that's left of our wine is the dregs, but Robin's story isn't finished. "And yet it didn't end there," she sighs. "Faison escaped to a boat where he was holding my mother hostage. My father tracked him to the boat, and he might have freed Mom had the WSB not—[128]

"So, yeah," Robin concludes. "Founder's Day. Not my favorite holiday."

[122] Lucy's note: Father to business-minded daughter Julia and giving-the-business-minded daughter Brenda.

[123] Lucy's note: My friend Dominique's domineering husband and all-around skeev. Would-be parents, please know forthwith: if you name your son "Leopold," you are surely sentencing him to an early doom courtesy of an S and M act gone awry.

[124] Says Tracy Q, "Not an actual lord, just your average English con artist."

[125] Editor's note: Which explains the sinking of the S.S. *Tracy*. With ELQ on its heels, the Quartermaines took the advice of advisor Paul Hornsby to sell the cannery. They were unaware Paul was really in the pocket of the Cartel, forced to do their bidding when they poisoned his daughter.

[126] Editor's note: Chiefly, Robert Scorpio and Anna Devane, with the help of PCPD honcho Sean Donely.

[127] Editor's note: Tiffany Hill is the star of such B movies as *Toxic Kiss of the Mutant Beetle Woman*, *The Prickling*, and *Lady Yeti v. Santa's Elves*.

[128] Editor's note: Robin's account gets cut off, redacted by representatives of the WSB. The best information we can provide is that Robert Scorpio, Anna Devane, and Cesar Faison were all lost at sea, presumed dead—though, as happens in Port Charles, all three would live to see another day, though it would take years before any of them resurfaced; long years of grieving for their friends and family.

I always say that the best way to see any city is in the back of a chauffeured limousine—or better yet, by helicopter![129] Alas, some of us have budgets, and we all hit rough patches.[130] So, for economy-conscious travelers, I've gone to the trouble of putting together a slew of tours that'll only cost you nothing but the indignity of being seen in sturdy footwear: walking tours! Port Charles is an eminently walkable city.[131] You'll find these themed routes designed to bring Port Charles's history to life—and maybe even put you in the path of some of its most adventuresome citizens. So tie your laces tight and book an appointment for a post-walk pedicure and foot massage. A-hoofing we shall go!

[129] Discover your destination from the air! Charter a ride on SHORE-line Whirlybird Tours! SHORE-line has branches throughout the United States and abroad, like in far-flung, exotic Santo Moro! Owned and operated by marine pilot Colton Shore, a tour with SHORE-line is sure to rate among your favorite vacation memories! Call 716-555-SOAR to book a flight today! (Editor's note: Colton Shore is our writer Lucy's first cousin. Readers should keep in mind that Shore's safety record is not without blemish. Mob heiress and oft-committed Olivia Jerome once commandeered his chopper in a daring escape from justice, resulting in a mountaintop crash-landing that nearly cost pilot and passenger their lives. As such things happen, they later fell in love!)

[130] Editor's note: As has Lucy, having lost not one but two different cosmetics companies to a variety of corporate takeovers and other calamities, such as a lawsuit over tainted makeup.

[131] Editor's note: In fact, walking is recommended. Though Mayor Quartermaine and the PCPD is working hard to reduce traffic, fatal car accidents are shockingly commonplace. Best to avoid Route 31 at night.

Our world-renowned hospital may have put Port Charles on the map with its many tales of limbs preserved and lives saved, but one study[132] shows that simply living here increases one's life expectancy well beyond the national average. There's something about Port Charles that has people coming back . . . even from the dead![133] The thought of everlasting life might put a spring in your step or a chill down your spine. I'm inclined to the latter, having personally encountered my share of the living dead.[134] So my advice is to undertake any of the following tours on the most appropriate holiday, Halloween—the one day every year when girls can be zombies, boys can truly be themselves, and Bobbie Spencer can wear both of her two faces at once.

Start getting around Port Charles by getting to know the subjects of some of its most miraculous recoveries.

[132] Editor's note: The study referenced was conducted by the tabloid newspaper *The Invader*. Asked to provide the data supporting their study, the publisher said they'd get back to us. Follow-up calls have not been returned.
[133] Editor's note: While true that on a number of occasions some residents have been presumed dead only to be proved not so, there exists scant evidence that any resident has actually been reanimated after the cessation of life.
[134] Editor's note: From time-to-time, Lucy has made claims of a clutch of vampires inhabiting Port Charles. At least one such claim landed her committed to the New York State Penal Psychiatric Institute at Ferncliff.

PIER 52

Start your tour on the industrial waterfront. Pier 52 is now closed to the public but can be accessed via a gap in the chain-link fence that would attempt to ward off all but those most determined intriguers.[135] Be sure to visit in the morning, when the drunks have all turned in, the brack glistens in the sunlight, and the odor is at its least funky. If you can take your eyes off the horizon for a moment, you may spot the remnants of a dark stain on the wooden planks. This would be the mark left by the blood of "Stone Cold" Jason Morgan, longtime associate and enforcer for reputed mob boss Sonny Corinthos. Jason has survived a number of close calls,[136] but none closer than at this spot. It was here that international terrorist and walking split-end Cesar Faison[137] caught Jason by surprise, shooting him in the back and kicking his body into the harbor like a barrel of toxic waste.

Upon learning of Jason's fate, his true love, sometime salvage diver Sam Morgan, donned her wet suit and braved the murk in an attempt to save him, just as he had saved her so many times. But there was no trace of him. His body was never found and he was declared dead.[138] In 2014, an amnesiac came to Port Charles whose DNA matched that of Jason's—though his face did not. Jason's friends and family accepted this man as the person they'd known and oh so terribly missed.

But three years later, fate stepped in yet again when the real Jason Morgan—with face and memories (mostly) intact—turned up a captive in a Russian plastic surgery clinic![139] Jason made his way back to Port Charles, crashing through the skylight of the Metro Court Hotel restaurant and thwarting the kidnapping of his erstwhile wife, Sam, who had since gone and married his twin, thinking it was him![140] Sam's husband turned out to be Jason's identical twin brother,[141] and the event known as "The Jasoning" began!

> *. . . visit in the morning, when . . . the odor is at its least funky*

[135] Editor's note: The publisher does not condone trespass or any other lawbreaking activity. But in the case of visiting the industrial waterfront, everyone does it. And the police seem to have better things to do than patrol this area.

[136] Jason has crashed his motorcycle; lost a head-to-trunk battle with a tree; been shot too many times to count in too many locations to name; suffered brain damage; and survived brain surgery, terrorist attacks, deadly influenza outbreaks, storms at sea, desert island strandings, slaps, Nurses Ball comedy routines, and many years of friendship with Carly Corinthos.

[137] Disguised as Anna Devane's on-again, dead-again paramour, Duke Lavery.

[138] Editor's note: An understandable if rash decision.

[139] Lucy's note: Maybe he hadn't paid his bill? Alas, St. Petersburg is not a stop on this tour, but notable nonetheless because those Quartermaines have always reminded me of Russian nesting dolls, hiding behind each other in plain sight.

[140] Editor's note: Rumor has it Tiffany Hill is pitching herself as Sam in a film rendering of the Morgan twin drama.

[141] Lucy's note: A surprise to everyone.

QUARTERMAINE MANSION LIVING ROOM[142]

Visiting the next location on our tour may require some ingenuity—or a sizable donation to General Hospital. The Quartermaine estate is one of the main epicenters of drama in our community.[143] Mistress of the house Monica isn't known to open her arms to just anybody—except perhaps her sister-in-law's son, then a sinewy, strapping young tennis pro[144]—so you'd best show up with a good excuse or a failing heart.

Once you get inside, take a look in the living room. Not for the chintzy decorating, but to steep in the history. It was here in 2012 that prodigal son A. J. Quartermaine reunited with his Mommy Dearest after seven years of presumed death. In 2005, wily Monica revived A.J. after he nearly perished at the hands of his Dr. Asher Thomas.[145] Since it looked like A.J. was going to be sent to prison for shooting Alan and kidnapping Michael, Morgan, and Kristina, Monica asked Steve to help her fake A.J.'s death. Of course, just two years after A.J.'s triumphant return to Port Charles he was dead yet again . . .[146]

[142] Located at 66 Harbor View Road. For a full tour of the house, please see the section entitled "The Quick and the Quartermaine."

[143] Editor's note: This is saying a lot, given that Port Charles has also been held ransom by an upper-crust English con artist who possessed the cure to a lethal strain of simian-spread encephalitis; criminal mastermind Jerry Jacks pulled a similar dirty trick in 2012 by contaminating the city's water supply with a deadly pathogen. Says Lucy, "The cleanup from the pathogen episode involved replacing all the pipes in Port Charles. Now our tap water is among the tastiest supplies in the country! Thank heaven for silver linings."

[144] Said Skye Q, "I hear Monica gave him her backhand to his backside, and he taught her his trick shot."

[145] Editor's note: Though not entirely substantiated, clues suggest psychiatrist Dr. Asher Thomas targeted A.J. to escape ongoing blackmail over an attempt made on Jason Morgan's life in 1996 while he languished in a coma. Unaware that A.J. survived and was spirited away by his mother, Dr. Thomas used hypnosis to pin A.J.'s death on his own son, Michael. "Just one of a multitude of reasons why Michael is such a mess," says his great-aunt Tracy. Lucy has this to say about the treatment of mental health in Port Charles: "GH gets a lot of things right. Psychiatric care is probably not one of them (my ex-husband excepted). If you think you need therapy, you're better off picking up a hobby."

[146] For now.

SECRET UNDERGROUND LABORATORY UNDER GENERAL HOSPITAL[147]

Round out this tour by dropping by General Hospital—just make sure you tell a loved one where you're going because the trip is neither easy nor safe. Sidle past security to take an elevator to the basement. Follow the signs for the morgue, then slip by to the boiler room. Somewhere inside is a hidden passageway[148] that, if unearthed, leads deep into the bowels of the earth—all the way to a secret underground laboratory well below GH (a laboratory that long housed the cryogenically frozen form of Mikkos and Helena Cassadine's favorite son, Stavros). Stavros might have died from injuries sustained in a 1983 fight with Luke Spencer at the Port Charles mayoral

mansion[149]—were it not for his mother's quick thinking. She had Stavros placed into stasis until technology was developed to revive him, then extorted Dr. Tony Jones[150] to do the reviving. Stavros awoke with an ax to grind, and he'd swing it at anyone bearing the last name Spencer. His awakening was brief but bloody. He killed poor fashion designer Chloe Morgan before eventually falling into a seeming bottomless pit. Unfortunately, this pit must've come equipped with an air bag, because Stavros survived to live again—and die and live and die again!

By now I'm sure you've cottoned to my general lack of faith in the psychiatric community.[151] I could fill a book with the head cases who've haunted Port Charles. I'll fill a few pages instead. Come with me on this walking tour of some of Port Charles's most legendary lunatics and amnesiacs. Nothing like a brush with involuntary commitment to make you feel pretty good about your own life. And for the purposes of full transparency, yes, it is true that I have seen the inside of a padded cell once or twice.

But since going on the lithium, I haven't seen a vampire. Hooray for Big Pharma! If only mood-altering drugs had the same effects on the subjects of our next tour. Let's take a step into their straitjacket . . . I mean shoes of each individual on their "journey."

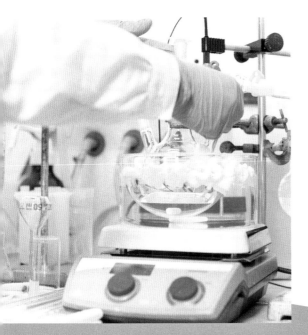

---

[147] 6065 Central Avenue, subbasement.

[148] Editor's note: Originally this lab was accessed only via an elevator that itself could only be boarded from the roof of GH. Years after the lab was sealed off, crazy-eyes Olivia Jerome embarked on a quest to locate the site of the lab, convinced the very ground it was built upon could restore Duke Lavery to life. It was Olivia who discovered a second entry point via the tunnel from the boiler room. Lot of tunnels in Port Charles!

[149] Yes, Luke Spencer was once elected mayor. What's that you say? A criminal, elected to office? Since when does that happen?

[150] Lucy's note: Tony, dear Tony. Another of my exes; he died of that encephalitis outbreak in 2006. But I know he's looking down from heaven, proud of the man his son Lucas has grown up to be; and hopefully proud that I finally grew up, too.

[151] Says Kevin C, "Don't worry, we don't have a lot of faith in you, either."

A WALK DOWN LOST-MY-MARBL

1242 ELM STREET

Begin your tour on the leafy lanes of the Brownstone District. The edifices lining the eight square blocks of this historic neighborhood are all modeled on the stately town houses so common to parts of Manhattan and Brooklyn. It was at one such home in the fall of 2014 that a particularly grotesque crime was carried out. A very pregnant, very loathed Ava Jerome was hiding out from her unborn baby's father, Sonny Corinthos, who was after her[152] for having murdered his ex, *Crimson Magazine* editor in chief Connie Falconeri, only to be discovered by Nina Reeves.

Nina—who in a twist of fate would later go on to replace the murdered Connie as editor in chief of *Crimson*—was unhinged. She'd spent upwards of twenty years in a coma after her mother, Madeline, injected her with a near-fatal dose of antidepressants in a half-baked scheme to abort Nina's pregnancy, thus keeping her own grandchild from inheriting a fortune she wanted for herself. Nina lost not only her baby to the coma but

her sanity as well. She awoke hell-bent on revenge against her husband, Dr. Silas Clay, whose long-ago affair with none other than Ava Jerome was what got the ball rolling on Nina's misfortune. By the time she came up on Ava that Halloween at the brownstone, Nina was wound tight—and wielding a drug capable[153] of inducing labor. Well one injection leads to another, and soon Ava was on her back and pushing with Nina's careful coaching. "Nina told me not to worry," says Ava. "She had experience delivering babies in difficult circumstances. Why, she had to reach in and pull one out by the hoof. That's when I realized the only baby she'd ever delivered was a horse."

Ava's daughter Avery was nevertheless delivered without incident—unless you count Nina then kidnapping the baby to Toronto. Fear not, Avery was returned to mother, and Nina eventually got the help she needed at a mental institution, where she met our next subject . . .

HEATHER WEBBER

The first stop on the train to Cuckooville is at a onetime workplace of the gal who never really had a full bag of marbles to lose.[154] Heather Webber's many bouts of madness have

---

[152] Says Sonny's lawyer Diane Miller, "Of course he was 'after her'; he wanted to ensure her safety during a demonstrably difficult pregnancy. That's exactly the kind of caring, thoughtful man any woman would want to have 'after' her."

[153] It should be noted that Port Charles area pharmacists have rather loosey-goosey standards for best practices.

[154] Editor's note: Lucy is not qualified to make a medical diagnosis. But trial records and state psychiatric documents confirm that clinically speaking, Heather Webber is cray cray.

taken her all over the place, like her escape to New York City. There, she sold her baby (by dreamboat Dr. Jeff Webber) for a measly $180, which she then attempted to parlay into a modeling career (yeah, right!) only to nearly get sucked into a seedy porno, and finally return to Port Charles where she'd sell Jeff on the story their baby had been stillborn, not auctioned off. But this is a tour of Port Charles, not New York City's outer boroughs, so we'll focus on Heather's hometown antics.

Located at 66 Paulson Street, you'll find a nondescript colonial; the former home of Diana and Dr. Peter Taylor. After her stint in New York City, Heather returned to Port Charles and sought out the Taylors, who had unwittingly adopted her baby. Unaware of Heather's connection to their son, "P. J.," the Taylors hired Heather on as a nanny. The Taylors were rattled when Heather got too close for comfort to P. J., eventually firing her. Heather responded with a scheme to drive Diana insane and wheedle custody of her own son.

The coup de grace had Heather dose Diana's iced tea with LSD. But you know what they say about "best-laced plans." So, along came little P. J., whose single turn of a lazy Susan had Heather obliviously drinking her own poison! Her resultant hallucinations forced husband Jeff to commit her to our next stop, Heather's home away from home, the Pine Circle Sanitarium.[155] Heather's obsession didn't end in Pine Circle. When Diana was murdered, Heather framed Jeff's virginal love, Anne Logan, for the crime by writing Anne's name in Diana's blood.

Either she didn't know or didn't care how hard it is to get blood out from underneath fingernails. Heather would go on to be linked to several more murders and various other crimes, like keeping a catatonic Laura Spencer cooped up in the Quartermaine attic, forcing LSD[156] on at least two other women,[157] and attempting to jump off the roof of General Hospital with Jason and Sam Morgan's baby son in tow. Who knows what the future has in store for this lady, who has yet to encounter a straitjacket she can't Houdini herself out of?

---

[155] Yet another Port Charles mental health facility, Pine Circle is located at 37 Red Post Road.

[156] Lucy's note: Or was it acid? I'm not sure, and I really don't want to ask Heather.

[157] One of whom was her son Steve's girlfriend, Olivia Falconeri. Says Olivia (now with the last name Quartermaine, courtesy of her marriage to Ned), "I lived with Heather's bad trip for ages. It had me seeing devils, dogs, and purple rain."

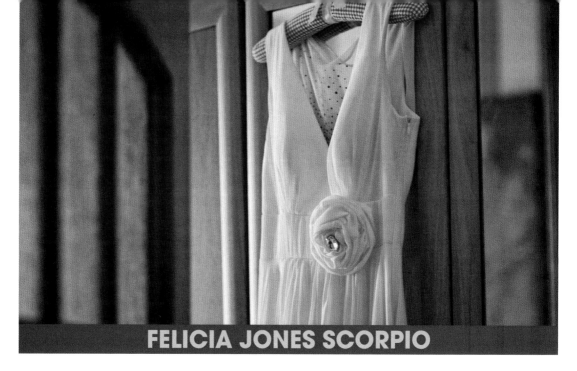

FELICIA JONES SCORPIO

My friend Felicia is one of those people who always has to top everyone; that pal in high school who turns around and tries out for the Olympics right after you tell her you're going out for the cheerleading squad. Not only was she once deemed to have had the highest hair in Texas, but she also suffered from not one but two bouts of amnesia. The first time was after a motorcycle accident endowed her with the identity of a charismatic carnie named Phoebe.

But Felicia couldn't remain anyone other than herself for long—not while under the spell of my ex-brother-in-law, the hunky, one-hit wonder, pop-singer-turned-PCPD sleuth-turned WSB agent Frisco Jones. Frisco and Felicia were the ultimate on-again/off-again lovers; it was after their final split that she crossed paths with perhaps the deadliest non-mob–related murderer ever to hit Port Charles, Dr. Ryan Chamberlain.[158] Felicia's instincts—never great to begin with—were not operating at their best when she struck up a friendship with Ryan. They were still off their game when she failed to immediately get help after witnessing him take an ice pick to a woman; and by "take" I don't mean "deliver."

Instead, she ran all the way from Texas to Port Charles. Ryan caught up with her just steps from a reunion with her family and doped her with a drug that induced Amnesia #2. He then proceeded to woo her, despite her lack of interest. Take a hike up to Cedar Mountain and you may find the cabin where his attempt at romance—presenting her with a wedding dress—finally jogged her memory. If ever self-defense is warranted, it's when a man says, "Here, try this on. I got it for you special." Felicia fought Ryan off, stabbing him no more times than required (but she *still* got sent to the loony bin). It was only after a concerted effort by Felicia's friends and family, led by Mac Scorpio, that the truth finally came out. Now, thanks to Mac, both her head and her heart are healed. Who knows what will next trigger Mrs. Scorpio? All good things come in threes. . . .

[158] Lucy's note: Also a former brother-in-law of mine. Suffice it to say, I much prefer Frisco and all his crazy hairstyles to Ryan's bloodlust.

66 HARBOR VIEW ROAD

Our next stop takes us back to the Quartermaine estate. But this time you won't have to get in good with the family or slip through the iron gates. Just down the road from the entrance is a tree stump, all that remains of a once stately old oak before it was uprooted and mulched for the grave offense of existing. The tree that once stood is partly responsible for turning former golden boy **Jason Quartermaine** into dark knight **Jason Morgan**. Yes, him again. You'll read Jason's name from time to time because the man is a lightning rod for disaster, which makes him such a scintillating subject!

It was on a cold night in 1995 that Jason's troubled big brother, A.J., got drunk and swiped in-law Lois Cerullo's car. Jason jumped into the passenger seat in order to prevent disaster. But disaster struck just the same when A J. ran his car into the offending tree. Jason was thrown from the car and suffered a gruesome head injury.[159] Cousin Ned came upon the scene and quickly sized up the situation. He collected a relatively unharmed A.J.[160] and delivered him to the care of butler Reginald, called 911, and returned to Jason, who betrayed only the barest signs of life. Soon he was rushed to General Hospital and put under the care of Dr. Tony Jones. He would

eventually awake from his coma, but not exactly recover from his traumatic brain injury.

Jason Quartermaine went into GH . . . and Jason Morgan came out. The accident caused him to lose his memory.[161] This Jason could not live up to the expectations of his heartbroken family—nor did he wish to. He soon broke ties with all but his sweet adopted sister, Emily, and city saint, Lila, taking her maiden name as his own. As tends to happen in Port Charles, this strangely orphaned Jason found his way into the bosom of Sonny Corinthos, and a very bloody[162] bond was formed. Jason would never recover his memory; a debilitating state, to be sure, though the neurological damage did endow him with one advantage: the ability to approach very nearly any situation[163] with an eerie calm.[164]

---

[159] Always wear your seat belt!

[160] Says Tracy Q, "Unless you count the million or so brain cells he'd destroyed in the binge leading up to the crash."

[161] Chiming in again is Tracy Q, saying, "As well as all traces of a personality."

[162] Says Corinthos lawyer Diane Miller, "I can't possibly imagine what you mean by 'bloody.' Jason and Sonny enjoy a long-standing lucrative and law-abiding partnership."

[163] From assaults of all varieties to runaway Zambonis, and everything in between.

[164] Lucy's note: Definitely not a Quartermaine family trait. Those people are screamers, let me tell you . . .

THE QUICK AND THE

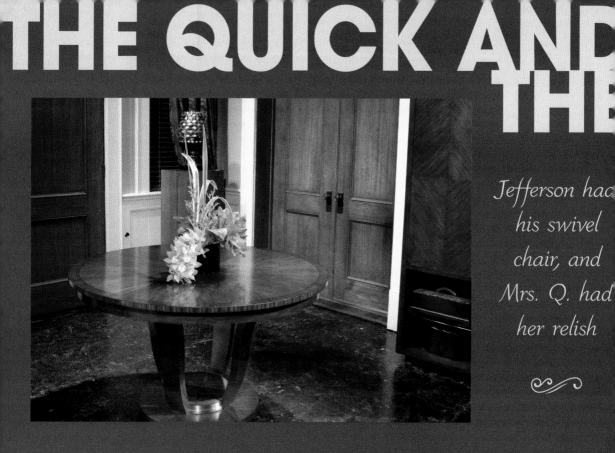

Jefferson had his swivel chair, and Mrs. Q. had her relish

T he Quartermaine mansion was bought by Alan, who always seemed to have too good a heart to be pure Quartermaine.[166] Alan bought the house in 1977 as a gift for his bride, Monica, when he decided to take a job at General Hospital. After Alan and Monica moved in, the rest of the Qs heard what a great place Port Charles was and, like the Thneeds in *The Lorax*, quickly came to town to build on their already large fortune. The mansion has been the home to everyone from supermodel Brenda Barrett, to loads of Spencers, Wards, Corinthoses, and, of course, many, many Quartermaines (with a few Falconeris thrown in for flavor).

Despite its numerous residents, Monica never lets anyone forget that the house is ultimately hers. Monica doesn't allow formal tours, due to "privacy concerns."[167] She does allow "limited viewing" house-and-garden walks in support of the Nurses Ball, but that's literally once a year. Lucky for us, though, retired maid Alice Gunderson has agreed to give us an inside, "unofficial tour" of the Q manor.

Even though he didn't build it, buy it, or even find it, it didn't talk long for Edward Quartermaine to appropriate the house. Edward seemed to want to run with other great American families like the Vanderbilts, the Astors, and the Kardashians; so he went about creating a family estate synonymous with grandeur. I'll let Alice give you the full dish, and maybe a few Grecian urns while she's at it:

[166] Comments Tracy Q, "Except when he was trying to blow up Monica."
[167] Editor's note: The views expressed by the author are strictly her own.

Howdy, folks, glad to hear you're visiting the most exciting city on the East Coast. If you're looking to really get the local flavor, there's no better place to than my former home away from home, the Quartermaine mansion. When Mr. Q first saw the house, he told his son it reminded him of Monticello and gave his blessing to use the family money to buy the place. Edward's research shows some of the bricks were manufactured in the same place as Jefferson's home. Makes sense that the Jeffersons and the Quartermaines would be connected in some way; both fancied themselves inventors as well as political patriarchs. Jefferson had his swivel chair, and Mrs. Q. had her relish.

GRAND ENTRY

The foyer is where more bombs have been dropped than in August at the multiplex. It features two huge bay windows that drench the room in natural light; all the better for dramatic entrances. Grand circular stairs are the centerpiece of the room and were sourced from cherry trees harvested from Mount Vernon itself. The round oak table in the center of the room is also said to have been acquired from the estate of George Washington.[168] House staff are instructed to have at least six bouquets of hothouse arrangements spread throughout the entry at all times. The flowers were to be changed as soon as they ceased to look fresh; and those stems wilted pretty fast by the amount of revelations witnessed.

Some of my favorite "overheard" moments in this room were when Sonny Corinthos confronted Carly about the paternity of her baby;[169] and Sonny and Brenda's non-wedding. Nothing will make you feel better about your own life than knowing a supermodel was left waiting in the rain for a man who is clearly not coming.

> *The foyer is where more bombs have been dropped than in August at the multiplex*

---

[165] 66 Harbor View Road
[168] Editor's note: Who can say?
[169] Sadly, Carly later suffered a miscarriage of this pregnancy.

THE LIVING ROOM

My mother always liked to say the living room is the neck that holds up the head of the house. That notion is particularly true in the Q mansion. Alan told me it was this room that convinced him to buy, because when the realtor showed it to him, the light reflected in such a way that a rainbow stretched across the room. He was poetic like that.

Located off the foyer, the living room is anchored by two grand couches facing each other, which I can only assume from personal experience ensure maximum potential for confrontation. While they have been reupholstered many times, the sofas themselves scream, "I'm not comfortable, so you'll be forced to sit up straight"—a good metaphor for the Q family themselves.

DEN

If the foyer and living room are where confrontations erupt, the den is where plots are hatched and misunderstandings multiply—aided by the attached terrace, which has the perfect acoustics for eavesdropping. The bookshelf against the wall is covered in pictures of all the Quartermaines.

My favorites are the ones of Lila and Edward from their wedding day; they looked at each other as if no one else existed. There's also a full bar, which is stocked solely with soft drinks; the Q's count several "Friends of Bill" amidst their ranks.

> *. . . the den is where plots are hatched and misunderstandings multiply . . .*

THE KITCHEN

I can't provide a description of this room, because no one but Cook Two is allowed inside. Bad things happen to those who attempt to gain entry.

GRAND SALON

Like the dining room, this formal room is rarely used. It contains a Steinway baby grand piano, which has heard the arrangements of everyone from Emily Quartermaine's amateur "Chopsticks" to Port Charles's own master pianist, Katherine Delafield.

LIBRARY

Right at the top of the steps is the entrance to the library, one of the must underutilized rooms in the house, and therefore one of the best places for teenage shenanigans. If I had a penny for every time Dillion Quartermaine snuck Georgie Jones up there, I'd have retired much sooner. The room features Renaissance and baroque tapestries that I think Alan got at a yard sale at Wyndemere. Much like the bookshelves in the den, the library is a room that is more about the appearance of knowledge then the actual acquisition of it. A.J. pretended to have memorized the complete works of William Shakespeare that his grandfather gave him for his sixteenth birthday, but I can tell you he enjoyed acting out the morals of those plays rather than actually reading them. Lila was a sucker for a good romance novel, which she'd hide beneath the spines of Jane Austen or Emily Dickinson.

DINING ROOM

One of the loveliest yet least used rooms in the house, as most holiday meals end up taking place in the den.[170] The room is mostly taken up by an antique oak table; when all its leaves are in place, it measures twenty-five-feet long. Another thing that sold Alan on the house is the chandelier that hangs over the table: it's from Schönbrunn Palace in Vienna, where Marie-Antoinette spent much of her childhood. A few months before his death, Alan Q commissioned Elizabeth Webber to paint a portrait of Marie to hang in the room.[171]

LILA'S ROSE GARDEN

This was Lila's favorite spot, and for good reason: it seemed to be the one place in that house that was always at peace. For a while, she had a policy: no talking, only pruning. But when residents like Tracy abound, such a policy can never last. Originally, the garden area was just a collection of weeds. But when his mother moved in, she sent for seeds from her friend (the queen at Buckingham Palace), to create a royal garden using descendants of Queen Victoria's own plants![172] So coveted were her rosebushes, that she donated several plants to the Port Charles Botanical Society, which today cultivates a Shakespearean garden in Lila's name. The mansion's gardeners still lovingly care for the bushes, and every year on Lila's birthday they send cuttings as gifts to lucky Port Charles residents still in the family's favor.

[170] Editor's note: While some families traditionally have turkey for Thanksgiving, for the Quartermaines (much to Cook Two's disgust) it's pizza, with extra anchovies. It has become a holiday tradition (along with singing an off-key rendition of "We Gather Together").
[171] Monica says: "I always suspect somehow Alan, deep in his heart, knew Elizabeth was carrying Jason's baby, and having her do that painting was a way of supporting the grandchild he thought he might never know."
[172] Editor's note: Again, this is unsubstantiated.

OLIVIA'S PUMPKIN PATCH

Ned Quartermaine's wife did not like the look of the tomatoes sold in town, so she decided to grow her own! What started as a few beefsteak stalks has turned into patches of basil, oregano, and pumpkins. She even has published a cookbook inspired by her garden-sourced creations, *Falconeris Know Fagioli.*[173] Her mother-in-law, Tracy, was driven mad by this "desecration of her mother's peaceful pruning, with this plebeian use of landscaping."

[173] Signed copies are available at the Metro Court gift shop for $19.99.

ROMAN POOL

Located to the right of the gardens and modeled after ancient Roman baths, the pool is tiled from ceiling to floor with images of Greek and Roman deities; some staff members swear Alan replaced their likenesses with his own. But I don't see it.

PORTRAIT GALLERY

The gallery is the room most people ask to see when visiting the estate. Located off the dining room, it's filled with pictures of family past and present, such as original matriarch, Martha, and patriarch, Edgar Quartermaine. The most notorious portraits include a replica of one of Tracy;[174] and one of Edward that some people say actually talked!

LILA AND EDWARD'S BEDROOM

Much like the man himself, this room was kept clear of any "nonsense." The room has remained its original hue of hunter green with wood trim for as long as I can remember. The only artwork in the room was won by Edward in a poker game; the subjects are all flower arrangements. After Lila's death, he told me that all knickknacks that served "no function except sentimentality" were to be removed where he'd never see them.[175]

Besides a dresser that held the same pair of pants in four different colors, is a giant oak bed modeled after the George Washington's. The enormous fireplace was barely used but always bore a framed photo of Lila and Edward. Cook Two told me that even after Edward's death, Monica has left the room untouched. Proving that some things never change, no one wants to deal with his wrath, supernatural or otherwise.

---

[174] Editor's note: It is rumored that this picture convinced Tracy of her father's love for her.
[175] Says Tracy Q, "Which usually meant my room."

TRACY'S BEDROOM

The most modern room in the house. When she moved in, Tracy decided to cover all of the original fixtures to give it her own spin. Tracy had a sound machine installed in all four corners of the room to continually play ocean sounds. When Luke moved in with her, a flat-screen television was installed, as well as a mini-fridge. Since her departure, this room has doubled as a guest room.

ALAN AND MONICA'S BEDROOM

The master bedroom, this room was modeled after the Doge's Palace in Venice (Italy, not California). The room is painted eggshell blue, and Monica has kept everything the same since Alan's death. As far as I know, his sweater-vests are still hanging in the closet waiting for him to wear them—which in this town is always possible. A Juliet balcony overlooks Lila's rose garden, and is perfect for late-night reflections.

ATTIC

For the storage of old toys, clothing, and, once, Laura Spencer.

THE CRYPT

The crypt was modeled after the Hollywood Forever Cemetery in Los Angeles. Alan made a pilgrimage there while in medical school to pay homage to some old movie stars[176] Alan had visited in his youth. Buried here are family members Justus Ward, Emily Bowen Quartermaine, and Lila, Edward, Alan, and A. J. Quartermaine. I've been told the crypt almost claimed Tracy herself when she hit her head and went to the great hereafter to defend her life, lest she be returned to the earth as a flatworm or Skye Chandler-Quartermaine's suckling babe.

[176] Says Monica Q, "Alan had a fascination with swashbucklers Rudolph Valentino and Douglas Fairbanks [who are buried at Hollywood Forever]. I think he was sure if he had been born a few decades earlier he would have made a dashing Robin Hood. That's why he loved performing at the Nurses Ball so very much."

GATE HOUSE[177]

This estate originally featured a home for the grooms and stableboys at the turn of the century. More recently it had been inhabited by Ned and his wife, Lois, until it burned to the ground.

BILLIARD ROOM

This room has always been a popular spot for the younger Quartermaines to relax and play both billiards and pool. The room is decorated with a variety of gaming themes and boasts a sixteenth-century Italian ceiling painted with scenes of palace life, as well as a Flemish tapestry from the 1400s.

P'S AND Q'S

Now that Alice has given you the run of the place, I thought I'd just help you get a little more acquainted with our town's Kennedys, starting with the source of their fortune, ELQ.

ELQ

For those coming to Port Charles for business, there is a good bet you'll be dealing with ELQ[178] or one of their many subsidiaries.[179] So, I'll do my best to give you the lowdown on the sordid history of the Edward Louis Quartermaine International company—and more importantly, its many storied captains of industry.

In 1978, after Edward Quartermaine followed Alan to town, he decided this was a fine place to relocate his company. Edward's first big venture was to try to find the Ice Princess diamond. After a decade of fortunes lost and found, Edward "died" and left everything to his grandson, Ned Ashton; years of tug-of-war for control of the company ensued between Ned, Alan, and Tracy. In 1991, ELQ was running at a loss, but Ned assured his family that an arriving cargo ship,

the SS *Tracy*, carried machinery that would revitalize their cannery and make them tons of money.

Unbeknownst to Ned, an environmental group called the Greenbelts were rallying to protest the arrival of the ship that they believed was also carrying toxic chemicals. Like the lady she was named after, the SS *Tracy* exploded en route to dock. The incident made Alan and Monica realize neither Ned nor Tracy could be trusted at the helm of ELQ.

Edward returned, revealing he'd merely been taking a long vacation in Bermuda. He resumed control of the reigns at ELQ but became obsessed with the idea of legacy and promised to bequeath the position of CEO to grandson A.J. if A.J. could bring his son, Michael, home.[180] And after marrying Carly, A.J. was appointed CEO. But A.J.'s rule was

---

[177] Before it burned to a crisp, the Gatehouse was located at 66 ½ Harbor View Road.
[178] 2457 Charles Plaza
[179] ELQ holdings have included L&B Records, Jacks Cosmetics, Lila's Kids Summer Camp, and Donely Shipping Company.
[180] Michael was being raised at this point by Jason and Carly.

short-lived; he was ousted after losing custody of Michael.

In 2001, Edward himself was given the boot in favor of his adopted granddaughter, Skye Chandler-Quartermaine. During Skye's tenure as boss, Jax sold his controlling interest in ELQ stock to Lila. Lila proved her mettle by anointing Edward co-CEO with Skye.

The next decade involved control of the company pinballing among Ned, Edward, Tracy, Alan, and A.J., as the family faced scandals ranging from arson to faulty condoms.

When Edward finally died—for real this time—his will was discovered to be as complicated as the man himself. Edward strew his stock amongst his progeny in varying amounts, depending on their generation. A combined 60 percent of his stock was left to his living grandchildren at the time: A.J., Skye Chandler-Quartermaine, Ned Ashton, and Jason Morgan;[181] a combined 30 percent went to his living great-grandchildren, Michael Corinthos, Lila Rae Alcazar, Brook Lynn Ashton, Maya Ward, and Danny Morgan; and 5 percent each to Edward's daughter-in-law, Monica Quartermaine, and maid—and tour guide extraordinaire—Alice Gunderson. Tracy's take was only a jar of Lila's Pickle-Lila relish.[182]

Now we come to my favorite part of the story—when I enter the scene. The shareholders could not agree on a CEO: Tracy or A.J.? But one person could turn the tide—Alan's former wife, holder of a 1 percent share of the company: *moi*! After securing Tracy's agreement to underwrite the Nurses Ball, I moved into the Quartermaine mansion and became co-CEO of ELQ (with Tracy). We can skip over the next bit, because, well it was not a good look on me.[183]

A.J. eventually became CEO once more, just in time for the United States government to seize all of ELQ's assets. While watching the company slip away, Tracy remembered the bottle of Lila's relish, and is struck by the grand idea to save the company by relaunching the brand that once took the country by storm. The Quartermaine hive-mind proved to be a thing, because at the same time A.J., Michael, and the newly hired hand, Duke Lavery, hit upon a similar notion. Now all anyone had to do was determine the formula for the relish recipe (frustratingly not on the container itself).

A.J. went so far as to have General Hospital lab technician Ellie Trout identify reverse-engineer the recipe, only to have Tracy steal the results. This game of capture the CEO flag went on for quite a while, at one time climaxing in a food poisoning incident via tainted relish—that unfolded on a live network television talk show, *The Chew*.

The next changing of the guard occurred in 2016, when Drew Cain[184] became the majority shareholder of ELQ and put Michael Corinthos in charge. By the time this guide is published, a new CEO could be anyone's guess; it could be you!

As a special treat, an anonymous source whose name rhymes with Bolivia, found in the Quartermaine Library, nestled in the pages of *Jane Eyre*, a handwritten recipe for relish. Is it the Pickle-Lila[185] recipe? Trademark infringements keep us from calling it exactly that, but do a taste test for yourself and decide:

PICKLE-LILA

INGREDIENTS

3 lbs. cucumbers, peeled and diced
1 large yellow onion, diced
1 small red bell pepper, diced
1 small green bell pepper, diced
3 cloves garlic, minced
¼ cup salt
3 cups white vinegar

1 cup sugar
2 teaspoons dill
1 tablespoon mustard seeds (try to find the
  yellowest ones you can)
2 teaspoons celery seeds
½ teaspoon turmeric
3 bay leaves

As I'm told, the "Iron Lady," Maggie Thatcher, once said, "If you want something said, ask a man. If you want something done, ask a woman." This quote is especially true around these parts, where ladies have pretty much saved the day in the face of every kind of disaster. Grab your favorite women's studies major and come along on what is personally my favorite tour of the bunch.

AUDREY HARDY

Let's begin at the beginning. In the courtyard of General Hospital,[186] there exists a number of features designed to soothe the souls of the ailing and their loved ones, including a Zen garden and a small sculpture park. At the center of the park, there stands a statue of a woman giving succor to a sickly patient above a plaque bearing the words, HOW VERY LITTLE CAN BE DONE UNDER THE SPIRIT OF FEAR.[187] The woman represented by the statute is one of GH's best-known luminaries, Audrey Hardy (née March).

Audrey retired in 2006 from her role as head nurse after a thirty-year career spent in service to Port Charles's sick and needful. Although lately Audrey's primary job is doling out TLC to her three great-grandchildren,[188] in her day she was about as indomitable as they come. For example, Audrey was determined to create a family with her husband, GH's chief of staff, Steve. But many failed attempts to conceive the old-fashioned way led Audrey to take matters into her own hands. She bucked the antiquated patriarchal rules that demanded a husband's consent to artificial insemination and underwent the procedure in secret!

Later, restless Audrey found herself not content to limit her lifesaving efforts to Port Charles. She fearlessly traveled to Vietnam at the height of the war to assist children orphaned by the conflict. Audrey was then and remains now a shining example of all that Port Charles's women are capable of.

> *If you want something done, ask a woman*

---

[186] 6065 Central Avenue

[187] Editor's note: Quotation attributed to nurse Florence Nightingale.

[188] In addition to being mother to Cameron, Jake, and Aiden, Elizabeth followed in her grandmother Audrey's footsteps: she is one of GH's most highly regarded nurses.

CATACOMBS

After exploring GH's sculpture park, stop by the PC Adventures Outfitter[189] to rent out their Catacombs kit—complete with a helmet with headlamp, waterproof clothes, kneepads, gloves, nonslip close-toed shoes, and (most important) a map of the underground. It's everything you'll need to explore the vast system of caves and natural passages that honeycomb Port Charles underfoot. The catacombs have long been exploited by Port Charles's seedier[190] set in order to move goods and do bad.

It was down here that the woman who puts the *b* in "bitch,"[191] one Bobbie Spencer, revenged herself[192] upon the one who did her wrong, preppy mobster wannabe Damian Smith.[193] Though married to stand-up guy Tony Jones, Bobbie found herself the object of Damian's romantic overtures.[194] Eventually, she gave in to his wandering hands and lost herself in a tawdry affair[195] that ended when Bobbie realized she was just Damian's plaything.[196] She lured him to the catacombs and cut the power, announcing to him that he was in a hell of her making. Damian bumbled around in the dark and whoops broke his back, only to be rescued by Lucky Spencer's French mastiff, Foster. Bobbie's marriage recovered (for a time; it turns out Bobbie is not nearly as forgiving of marital indiscretions as Tony was), and so did Damian—but he had learned his lesson: never slight a Spencer!

---

[189] 944 Black Duck Boulevard

[190] Says Corinthos lawyer Diane Miller, "I'm sure you are not referring to my client; such a claim is libelous and would be met with immediate legal action."

[191] Says Bobbie S, "And you put the *l* in loose!"

[192] Asks Bobbie S, "Are you going to tell your readers exactly WHY I felt compelled to get even?"

[193] Lucy's note: I was just getting to that!

[194] Says Bobbie S, "Still waiting . . ."

[195] Says Bobbie S, "I held out for a long time!"

[196] Says Bobbie S, "It's clear Lucy won't give you the full context, so I will. See, my affair with Damian would never have occurred were it NOT for Lucy's sordid greedy streak. Lucy wanted Damian's ELQ shares, and he wanted *hers*—plus a night in bed with her. I have a feeling Damian had stock in antibiotics. So they made a wager. Damian could earn his winnings if he successfully seduced a woman of Lucy's choosing—and she chose *me*. When Damian came sniffing around I—perhaps somewhat naively—elected not to send him packing. His father was my brother Luke's original mortal enemy! Like any good sister, I thought I could gather intelligence Luke could use to protect his family. I didn't expect to actually fall for smarmy Damian. Although I should have expected nothing less from Lucy. No amount of rehab will burnish her image; skank always shines through."

PORT CHARLES POLICE DEPARTMENT

The great big art deco building located at 1438 Central Avenue is a marvel of design—and it's also a marvel that it's still standing. When disaster strikes,[197] it is the first responders of the PCPD who answer the call. All officers of the law go above and beyond, putting their lives on the line every day to protect us mere citizens. But some of the jobs they undertake are more dangerous than others; few of them are more dangerous than going undercover to infiltrate a murderous crime family.

But that's exactly what DEA agent Jordan Ashford did when she embarked on a years-long effort to construct just the right kind of background that would entice the interest of Julian Jerome. Jordan set herself up as the perfect right-hand woman—all the better to take down the Jeromes from within . . . and learn which shadowy figure was secretly calling the shots.[198] To make matters all the trickier, Jordan's assignment took her into direct conflict with Shawn Butler, enforcer[199] for alleged Jerome rival Sonny Corinthos—father of her son, T. J.! Jordan got the job done, even though she had to send Shawn to prison in the process. And when the operation was finally complete, Jordan was awarded with a new job, becoming the first black woman to lead the PCPD as commissioner!

[197] Editor's note: It strikes often and with gusto.
[198] Editor's note: Luke Spencer, fractured by a long-ago psychological trauma. Pipes Lucy, "Remember what I said about mental health in Port Charles?"
[199] Says Corinthos lawyer Diane Miller, "Enforcer? What is an enforcer? Shawn was merely Sonny's assistant, 'enforcing' memos."

62

AVA JEROME GALLERY

Drop in at the Ava Jerome Gallery[200] for a gander at all the latest in contemporary art[201]—and a glimpse at Port Charles's very own Lady Macbeth (just switch out the twisted spousal dynamic for a sibling one). Ava[202] is thought to have been at the center of many of Port Charles's most shocking crimes since her arrival in town in 2013, the secret partner to her brother Julian. Then going under the name of media magnate Derek Wells,[203] Julian was using his revamped identity as a cover while relaunching the Jerome criminal syndicate.

As dastardly as Julian was, he was nothing compared to—or without the assistance of—sister Ava. When Sonny Corinthos's girlfriend Connie Falconeri discovered Julian's true identity, it was Ava who shot her down. When Sonny sought to avenge Connie's

death, it was Ava who shifted the blame onto A. J. Quartermaine, whom Sonny then murdered![204] Ava has since been linked to disgraced former DA/murderer Paul Hornsby, as well as to the tragic death of Sonny and wife Carly's only biological son, Morgan—with whom Ava previously carried on a long and torrid affair![205] For Ava's many crimes, she was punished with a short stint in Pentonville but having her face burned off. But since then she's undergone a transformation, winning the love of a man previously married to God and reconstructive surgery.

Will the "new look" Ava last? Only time will tell—but if I were a betting woman,[206] I'd say it won't be long before Ava finds herself in a situation requiring *killer* instincts.

[200] 139 Broadway

[201] Says noted collector Richard Halifax, "Prices are reasonable, the quality without par."

[202] Editor's note: One of several of Victor Jerome's children born out of wedlock, this one to mistress Delia Ryan.

[203] Lucy's note: It helps when you've undergone face-changing plastic surgery and a complete identity redo thanks to witness protection program largesse.

[204] Lucy's note: Diane? You there, Diane? Care to chime in? I'm waiting!

[205] Lucy says: "Before engaging in a onetime Quartermaine crypt tryst with Morgan's own father! I mean, there's exhibitionism, and there's having sex in front of Mother Quartermaine. For that alone Ava ought to have been struck down."

[206] Asks Bobbie S, "IF???"

...the Outback Bar & Club...
was treated to one of the most
eye-popping birthday celebrations...

5563 KING PLACE

Head to LiSy for the next stop on our tour of unsinkable women, the poke-bowl restaurant that was once the site of the Outback Bar & Club. It was here that I was treated to one of the most eye-popping birthday celebrations in Port Charles's memory—thanks to Lois Cerullo. As Olivia Falconeri has proved in recent years, you can take the girl out of Brooklyn, but you can't take the Brooklyn out of the girl.

And the same holds true for Lois. The first Bensonhurst broad to make waves in Port Charles, Lois was a music-act manager and childhood pal of Sonny Corinthos. Her first contact with Port Charles came due west in a Buffalo hotel, where she clashed with an amateur critic. His faint praise for the band she managed—the Idle Rich—resulted in her challenge to do better. Not one to back down, the man (who called himself Eddie Maine) climbed onstage and tore the roof off the bar. Lois promised right then and there to make the man a star—and then made him hers!

What Lois didn't know was that "Eddie Maine" was really Ned Ashton of the Quartermaine family! Ned kept up the charade for months, falling hard for Lois—all the while engaging in war over the fate of ELQ, a war that saw the family force him to marry town trollop Katherine Bell,[207] who possessed evidence incriminating Alan in the death of his friend Rhonda's abusive boyfriend, Ray Conway.

Soon after marrying Katherine, Ned stole away to Lois and married *her*, desperately keeping secret the fact that their marriage wasn't legal.[208] After figuring out the truth when she saw Ned on television, Lois set out to get even—and the perfect opportunity presented itself when Katherine's birthday rolled around. A humongous wedding cake was delivered to the party at the Outback . . . and from it popped a red bustier-clad Lois, who exclaimed, "Happy birthday, Mrs. Ned Ashton! From me—the other Mrs. Ned Ashton!" That night I had Katherine's cake and ate it, too! Brava, Lois!

[207] Scott B provides context: "Typically I add my weight in salt to any of Lucy's opinions on the fairer sex—they tend to stem from very jealous ground. But in this case, I have to get her back. Katherine was a lying user who was carrying on with Damian Smith while sidling up to me, trying to get a hold of my late wife Dominique's inheritance. She can rot."

[208] Says Brenda B, "I'd figured out the truth about Ned's double identity a while ago and begged him to come clean to Lois, who was by then my business partner and best friend. But he was determined to handle things his way. . . ."

3728 CENTRAL AVENUE, SUITE 308

You may be forgiven if having gotten this far you come to the conclusion that we Port Charlesers are perhaps a tad familiar with the inside of the PCPD jail cells. It is true that many of us—even the innocent—have spent a night or two behind bars for some often trumped-up reason. Some[209] might say this is due in part to an over-exuberance on the part of the PCPD; but here we'll focus on the reason we don't all stay behind bars: the efforts of one of Port Charles's most brilliant legal minds, Diane Miller. It is here in her offices at 3728 Central Avenue that Diane applies her vast knowledge of the legal system, intimate to defending her innocent clients—and perhaps some guilty ones, too.

Whether you're an accused scofflaw or stalker, Diane is your go-to woman, having employed both the tumor defense[210] and marry-the-prime-witness maneuver[211] to great success. Diane's number[212] is often the first one called when anyone in these parts is accused of anything. I'm sure no trouble will come to you during your visit to Port Charles—but best to have her number handy, just in case.

[209] Editor's note: Those "some" include Sonny Corinthos, Jason Morgan, Julian Jerome, Ava Jerome, Franco . . . the list goes on for pages and pages. . . .

[210] Editor's note: To keep artist Franco out of jail for his many crimes. Says Jason M, "If I had been around, that tumor never would've come out of Franco's head; he'd be buried with it still in his head." Adds Diane, "Not to be taken seriously. My client is a master of hyperbole."

[211] Editor's note: For client Sonny, when he stood accused of the shooting of Lorenzo Alcazar. Sonny's subsequent marriage to Carly prevented either from having to testify against the other.

[212] Call 716-555-LAWS for a free consultation and a coupon for fifty cents off a cup of Corinthos coffee at any Perks location!

ELM PARK

The fountains, hedgerows, and lush greenery of Elm Park make this spot a must for any Port Charles picnicker. But the beauty belies a dark truth. Like many secluded spots the world over, Elm Park is not very safe at night. Elizabeth Webber learned that the hard way.

"I was supposed to go to the PC High Valentine's Dance with Lucky. But something came up and I wound up going alone."[213] Elizabeth dawdled on her way, stopping in the park to look up at the stars. "I was wearing a new dress and my gram's bracelet. It was a beautiful night and I felt beautiful." She takes a deep breath and exhales. In a steady voice, she says, "And then a man grabbed me, dragged me into the bushes, and raped me."

When I decided to build this tour, I thought of the many hero women I've come to know in Port Charles. Some of them are heroes for things they've done; some for things they've

[213] Lucy's note: With Liz's permission, I spoke to Lucky to gather his memories of that night and everything that transpired as a result. Lucky has always been an expressive person. Even a thousand miles away, far across an ocean, he is unable to hide his sadness. "Liz is being kind. The thing that came up was me being insensitive, asking her sister to join us at the dance. I was supposed to be with her that night. But I wasn't. Not at first, anyway."

survived. Liz is both. I didn't know how to include her in this section without talking about her assault, so I decided to reflect her experience and achievements elsewhere. But the subject arose during our interview and she stopped me mid-sentence.

"I spent too many nights trying to bury what happened to me or pretend it out of existence. But it's a part of my history. It's a part of who I am. And it's no cause for shame. If by telling my story I help just one person, then it will have been worth it. I'd be proud to be one of your indomitable women, Lucy."

And so she is. Liz was only fifteen when she was raped. She showed a maturity well beyond her years when she put herself back together and reported the crime. Later she proved her mettle when she faced down her attacker. Armed with a gun, Liz might have killed him right then. Nobody would've blamed her. But instead she lowered her weapon and saw to it he went to prison. I can't imagine the spirit required of her to let that man live. But one day I hope to.

TOUR

WITH A TWIST

Believe it or not, I don't know everything there is to know about Port Charles. There are some residents who are better suited to showing you different parts of the city, and whose points of view might offer a different take on its rich history. So in case you've had enough of hearing from me[214] I've invited a bunch of friends[215] to weigh in with tours of their own. Get a load of Port Charles from these folks.

[214] Lucy's note: The editor made me say that. Who could ever have enough of *moi*?
[215] Lucy's note: As well as some people I don't like very much but are sure to get the job done.

RS

To start us off, please meet a woman I've known since she was just a glimmer in her father's eye. Lulu Spencer Falconeri is the daughter of Port Charles celebs Luke and Laura—and she's just as prone to drama as they are, which is why she volunteered to lead you through the following tour. Take it away, Lulu!

Says Lulu: Everyone loves a juicy revelation; and as an investigative reporter for the *Port Charles Press*, I'm obliged to give the people what they want. So for my entry to this guide, I'm taking you on a tour of the spots where Port Charles's secret children finally found their rightful place in the family—whether they wanted to or not.

THE ASIAN QUARTER

Like a lot of this country, our fair city bears the stains of the past embedded in our DNA and in our driveways.[216] For a long time Port Charles was a city divided by race. Black Port Charlesers lived in the Charles Street neighborhood, while many Chinese-Americans made their home in our very own Chinatown, the dismayingly named "Asian Quarter." It was as a result of an adventure that wound its way through the back alleys and herb shops of the Asian Quarter[217] that a girl who would grow up to become everyone's favorite[218] doctor, Robin Scorpio-Drake, first learned that her parents were none other than international superspies, Anna Devane and Robert Scorpio.

"For the first seven or eight years of my life, I was raised by a kindly woman whom I thought was my grandmother—Filomena Soltini," remembers Robin. "Throughout that time we were often visited by a gorgeous woman with a beautiful smile and bright, very sad eyes."

Anna remembers it, too. "Robin used to call me 'Luv.' I let her believe I was merely a friend of the family. She had no idea I was her mother, to say nothing of the reasons I'd long kept the nature of our relationship secret."[219] When little Robin overheard Anna and Robert discussing whether and when to clue her in to the truth, she took off.

"What can I say? I was a precocious kid."[220] Robin took a break from her deceitful parents, for a time hiding out in General Hospital—where she misplaced her favorite doll. The doll fell into the hands of an elderly resident of the Asian Quarter, who saw that its eyes had been replaced with missing black pearls, precious to his colleagues. Robin returned the eyes to their rightful owner, but not before they were both abducted by members of a rival faction, also hungry to possess the pearls.

Thus kicked off a serpentine escapade that finally ended with Robin reunited with Anna,

---

[216] Lucy's note: And she's not only talking about the stray shell casing from a mob shoot-out.

[217] Says Brad Cooper, "Just hearing those two words put together hurts my heart."

[218] Says Carly C, "Know-it-all? Busybody? Scold? All apply. Take your pick."

[219] Says former WSB spymaster Sean Donely, "Mainly to protect Robin from people who might use her against Anna. I'm ashamed to say that at one point in my life such a person might have been me." Robin scoffs when she hears what Sean told me. "I know Sean did some rotten things back in the day. But he'd never have hurt a hair on my head."

[220] Says Robin's husband, Patrick, "Runs in the family." Says Lucy, "I have a hunch he's referring to their daughter, Emma, who has been known to inspire trouble in some of our younger generation."

and the acknowledgment that they and Robert were a family. Though Anna and Robert have long since parted ways romantically, they are still very much a part of one another's lives and have formed one of the tightest family units I've ever known. The Asian Quarter maintains a distinct urban flavor, and though it has since diversified, one can still find many traces of its unique heritage in the pagodas and archways that dot the neighborhood. It's one of those up-and-coming neighborhoods where you can get great dim sum[221] and top it off after with a cannoli next door.

[221] Try the Noodle Buddha at 65 Mott Street. "Order the Phoenix and the Special," says Sam M. "And tell them JaSam sent you," adds Jason M.

THE HAUNTED STAR NIGHTCLUB

From the Asian Quarter, stroll west along the waterfront and you'll soon hit 100 Commodore Way. Walk down Pier 23 to berth No. 2 and you'll find yourself gazing up at a mammoth luxury yacht: it's the *Haunted Star*. Ask for the owner, Lulu. Yep, I'm captain of that lucky lady. Though at times I wish I wasn't.

Before the *Haunted Star* was mine, it was my parents'. And before it was theirs, it was owned by their greatest enemies, the Cassadines.[222] Given its roots, it makes a twisted kind of sense that the *Haunted Star* would serve as the backdrop for yet another revelation about my family. It was there that my brother from another mother[223] came into our lives. Ethan Lovett was a bartender at the *Haunted Star* during my father's third[224] attempt[225] to make a business[226] of it.[227] Mixology wasn't his calling, though. Ethan was a con artist who sought out Luke in the hope of honing his craft by an apprenticeship with

[222] The Cassadine family yacht was originally named the *Titan*. Luke and Laura rechristened it the *Haunted Star* after receiving it as a wedding gift. "The spoils of war," Luke calls it.

[223] Editor's note: Holly Sutton, an ex of both Luke's friend Robert Scorpio and Luke's look-alike cousin, Bill Eckert.

[224] Says Sam M, "I thought we were going to be partners on the first go-around. But that rat bastard and Skye Chandler-Quartermaine edged me out of my claim."

[225] Says Tracy Q, "He used its second grand opening to try to rob me blind."

[226] Says Alexis D, "I was acting DA at the time of Luke's third endeavor to make something out of that bucket of bolts. He'd partnered on the venture with the criminal Zacchara family, who in turn were using it to launder money. I shut down that eyesore posthaste."

[227] Snorts Luke S, "Women."

a master. It was Helena Cassadine who first observed the similarities between Dad[228] and Ethan,[229] speculating that they were father and son. Dad started seeing it, too.

I'm sure it also helped that Dad crossed paths with Ethan at a time when he and my brother Lucky had hit one of their rough patches. His antenna for substitute sons was on overdrive. After much back and forth about whether Ethan was Holly's son by Robert Scorpio or Dad, she came clean—on the boat,

no less. Fitting that Dad would learn about his secret kid in a casino,[230] since so many of his life decisions have been based on rolls of the dice.

Ethan eventually took his adventures on the road, but not before bonding with the extended Spencer clan. I keep a drink on the *Haunted Star* menu in his honor: "The Aussie Stowaway." Now let's move on to our next subject, all the while keeping things in the family. . . .

[228] Editor's note: *Another* Australian!
[229] Says Lucky S, "Like the way they take their whiskey." Once said Nikolas C, "And the stupid, scrunched-up look they get on their faces right after they drink it."
[230] Editor's note: The *Haunted Star* no longer operates as a casino. It is open for dinner and drinks nightly, rents out rooms, and may also be chartered.

THE GENERAL HOSPITAL PEDIATRIC WING

I don't mean to make this tour all about me[231] and my family, but there's just no escaping it: the Spencer family history is rife with secrets, and Ethan is not my only surprise brother. The first time the family underwent an unexpected expansion, it took place here,[232] where I was recovering from a bone marrow transplant to save my life from the ravages of aplastic anemia. I was just a baby. Lucky came into the room to keep me company and found a kid a few years older hovering over the crib. It was Nikolas Cassadine—our half brother. When I got sick, Stefan[233] Cassadine[234] saw an opportunity to fuse himself to our rapidly dysfunctioning clan.

Very quickly the truth came out that during our mother's captivity on Cassadine Island, Stefan's older brother forced himself on her, begetting Nikolas. She forged a friendship with Stefan, and he did his best to protect her from brutal Stavros, even helping her escape back to Port Charles, where she reunited with Luke, though she had to leave Nikolas behind in order to do it. She made a secret attempt to reclaim her son, but Helena stepped in, murdering Laura's mother[235] as a warning to never again come for Nikolas.

Eventually, Helena grew infirm[236] and Stefan was able to remove Nikolas from her influence, taking him to Port Charles—where his matching bone marrow provided just the healing elixir I needed. Nikolas and Lucky were at each other's throat for a long time before eventually calling a truce.

[231] "Ha!" chuckles Lulu's sometime best friend, sometime frenemy, Maxie Jones-West.
[232] 6065 Central Avenue, in case it hasn't already sunk in.
[233] Pronunciations vary. Luke S says, "I called him Steffin. He loved it." Bobbie S says, "I always thought it was Ste-FAWN."
[234] Says Luke S, his teeth grinding, "Yet another Cassadine obsessed with Laura."
[235] Editor's note: Dr. Lesley Webber. Happily—and like so many other Port Charlesers—Lesley's murder didn't take, either.
[236] Editor's note: Unhappily, Helena's infirmity didn't take, either. She was back in fighting-and-filleting form a few years later.

THE LAW OFFICES OF ALEXIS DAVIS[237]

Most of the criminally charged call Diane Miller for help—but only because Alexis Davis's time is at a premium. Three times voted Lawyer of the Year by the Port Charles Bar Association,[238] Alexis has a knack for helping her clients beat such charges as the illegal importation of coffee beans[239] and stalking.[240] Perhaps the biggest discovery made in her office was not of the legal but maternal variety. After a lot of false starts involving kids being born on the same day in New Hampshire,[241] Jason Morgan burst into Alexis's office and revealed the truth: the daughter that then sixteen-year-old Alexis thought died at birth on Mother's Day was her very nemesis, grifter and deep-sea salvage diver Sam McCall! The proof that cinched it was the answer to a question Jason asked of Alexis: Who is so perverse as to fool Alexis into thinking her daughter dead?

None other than her own dear, departed daddy: Mikkos. Sam and Alexis are a lot closer now than they were then. Both pull no punches when asked to opine on the other's selection of male companions.

[237] 149 South Main Street

[238] Editor's note: In spite of her many subversions of the very law she practices, including but not limited to attempted murder, murder, and posing as a butler with very bad fake facial hair.

[239] Says Diane M, "Sonny Corinthos is *my* client now, and there is nothing wrong with the importation of coffee beans—unless the beans are bad. You do not want to run afoul of me if I haven't had my morning jolt of Corinthos coffee!"

[240] Editor's note: Lucy may here be referring to the case of Kevin Collins. It was Lucy herself who brought Alexis to town, hiring her to defend Kevin after a break from reality had him thinking he was his own deranged twin brother, serial killer Ryan Chamberlain. Kevin went on to stalk poor beleaguered Felicia Jones before being brought to justice. Felicia refused to go along with the prosecution after Alexis proved Kevin was suffering PTSD from his mother's abuse and only needed a heavy dose of therapy. Says Lucy, "Again with the therapy! Although in Doc's case it worked out okay."

[241] Lucy's note: "New Hampshire being the American state where the Greco-Russo Cassadine clan send their kids to boarding school, because of course."

Since we're speaking of Jason,[243] why not drop by the Metro Court for our penultimate stop on the tour? Take a ride to the rooftop bar and restaurant for drinks at sunset. While you're ascending, pause and consider—you're standing in the scene of one of our more unusual paternity reveals.[244] While on a break from her roller-coaster romance with my brother Lucky, Elizabeth Webber enjoyed a night of bliss with leather-jacketed, stone cold mob enforcer[245] Jason. Later Liz discovered she was pregnant but decided for "many" reasons[246] not to tell anyone her tot's father was Jason. Nothing like being stuck in an elevator after a hostage crisis[247] to hasten truth telling.[248]

[242] 1420 Quartz Lane

[243] Lucy's note: The way some people (coughCARLYcough) around here talk, I have to wonder—if we're not speaking of Jason, are we really speaking at all?

[244] Editor's note: "Unusual" short of a Tiffany Hill talk show special (Tiffany Hill, star of such B movies as *Devil Deer, Devil Deer 2: Stag Night,* and *Devil Deer 3: Easy Does It*)

[245] Says Corinthos lawyer Diane Miller, "*Alleged* mob enforcer."

[246] Says Sam M, "But mainly just one. To keep Lucky sober."

[247] Editor's note: Jerry Jacks's

[248] Barks Carly C, "Or try to forever hitch herself to Jason's side. It didn't happen then, and it never will!"

SONNY CORINTHOS'S HOUSE[249]

Situated[250] amidst rolling Arcadian hills overlooking the lake, Sonny's house boasts killer views and the coveted final spot on this list because it involves Lulu's one and only, her husband Dante Falconeri. The Corinthos house has been the site of much breaking: the breaking of bread, glassware by the truckful, kneecaps, and the news that Sonny is the father of the undercover police officer he shot. Sonny had taken a shine to "Dominic Pirelli," the young man whose chutzpah won him a place in the organization and eventually a pivotal role in the inner circle. The rumor[251] goes that Sonny was devastated to learn that Dominic was really Dante—a cop sent to gather everything he could about Sonny, the better to finally putting together an airtight case against him. Alone in his house while ex-wife Carly and then-husband Jax were christening their daughter, Josslyn, Sonny shot Dante.

A moment later Dante's mother, Olivia Falconeri, is thought to have run in and imagined to have screamed that Sonny had just shot his own son! Eat your heart out King Lear.[252] Who needs a trip to England when we've got our own Shakespearean tragedies playing out right here?

[249] Lucy's note: For reasons you'll soon understand, Lulu declined to pen this final entry. This one's on me.
[250] 120 Shoreline Road; apocryphally known to some as Greystone Manor
[251] Spits Corinthos lawyer Diane Miller, "*Exactly!* This is all rumor! Detective Falconeri stated for the record that he accidentally shot himself! Lucy, I'll see you in court!"
[252] Adds Lulu, "I can joke about it because I'm family. Also because Dante and Sonny have put all that behind them. I think."

Here's teenaged Josslyn Jacks, daughter of Jasper "Jax" Jacks and Carly Corinthos, to open the dressing room door on the life of the world's littlest supermodel:

Brenda's footsteps for this book—though I'm still waiting for the Cartullo boots she promised in return![255]

Brenda was so many things to so many different people. Ask ten people and you'll

> *She's totally everything I want to be—minus the shaky sanity and extra-long sleeves*

I don't see much glamour when I look at Port Charles. Sure, my mother wears head-to-toe haute couture; yes, the Metro Court Hotel is also home to the fashion magazine *Crimson*; fine, my father and my stepfather both have private jets.[253] It's not that there's no glitz at all, it's that our streets are much better known for scrubs than for sequins. But from what I've heard whispered while listening from behind closed doors, my stepfather Sonny's ex Brenda Barrett was the most thrilling person[254] to ever step foot on the East Coast—and to think, for a long time she chose to set it in Port Charles. I was so excited when Lucy asked me to follow in

get ten different answers. To some, she's best known for her charitable side as a goodwill ambassador for the ASEC.[256] To others, she's a music industry icon, one of the original partners of upstart record label L&B. To a certain few, she's pure demon spawn.[257] There's not a person alive who doesn't know her as the Face of Deception and the spokesperson for Jax Cosmetics and global brand representative for Cartullo Couture! She's totally everything I want to be—minus the shaky sanity and extra-long sleeves. Can we all please agree never to let those come back?

---

[253] Says Jax J, "Yeah but only one of us actually knows how to fly his private jet."
[254] Says Brenda B, "Your daughter has taste, Carly."
[255] Lucy's note: Patience is a virtue kid!
[256] Alliance to Save Exploited Children
[257] Josslyn's note: My mother made me write that.

ELM STREET PIER[258]

The waterfront is romantic for so many reasons . . . the sea breeze . . . the clang of the harbor bells . . . the limited cell service so your parents can't text you to come home. It's also stop number one on our tour because it's where Brenda and Sonny first met! The way Sonny tells it, he saw Brenda struggling to carry a couple armloads of boxes.[259] Sonny, ever the gallant, always a sucker for a damsel in distress, beamed his dimpled smile her way and swooped to her rescue.[260] "I wanted nothing to do with him," says Brenda. "He was bad news."

"Sometimes bad news means new beginnings," Sonny told me, only to follow up with, "But if anybody ever tries a line like one of mine on you, run in the other direction. And then call me." Sonny and Brenda's romance began with a simple handshake. It got a lot more complicated.

[258] Where Elm Street meets the water.
[259] Josslyn's note: Brimming with high fashion, I'm sure.
[260] Says Brenda B, "The way I remember it was that he was overconfident and full of himself." Says Sonny C in response, "That's why she liked me."

LAKEWOOD LUXURY CARS

I guess the car dealership has changed hands a couple of times since Brenda paid it a visit on Valentine's Day in 1994. She was fresh off her first success as the Face of Deception and rolling in green, ready to put some of it to good use by buying herself a fast car. But it wasn't chrome and leather that engaged[261] her senses that day.[262] It was Sonny. "I had my eye on a foreign number. Something classy. Powerful. Prestigious. Something in British racing green.

And then along came Sonny. And he's telling me the car I've picked out for myself is not the one I really want. He tells me I should go for something flashy. Something that befitted my youth. Something *red*."[263] "A lot of other women might've taken offense at being told what's good for them. I saw it as a challenge. And I gave[264] as good as I got."[265] The dating commenced soon after that, and the drama was right behind.

261 Says Carly S, "I could puke."
262 Says Jax J, "Me too."
263 Josslyn's note: Oscar N is reading this over my shoulder. He wondered if it was just him or was it hot in here?
264 Says Brenda B, "And then of course I went and bought myself the red car."
265 Says Sonny C, "And then of course I went and bought myself the classy, prestigious car."

Brenda's modeling career was wildly successful—but not without turmoil. "Lucy was always tangled up in some fight over stock, who was in charge of what, stolen supplies, drug busts."[267] I'd wake up every day wondering whether I had a job to go to at all. And Lucy—God love her[268]—was at times more interested in her schemes[269] than in her business plan." I always thought models led these amazing, cosmopolitan lives. But Brenda makes it sound like a drag. "Sure, there was money. Yes, there was first-class travel all over the world to exotic locations. I can't deny it was exciting—but it was also 6:00 a.m. makeup calls, daylong shoots, tyrannical photographers, and never enough masseurs. In the back of my mind, I was always thinking that I needed to cultivate other opportunities."[270] And then fate scratched a chalkboard with one-inch[271] press-on nails.[272]

"I was looking for a capital infusion to take The Idle Rich to the next level," says music manager Lois Cerullo. "You know, elevate us from airport hotel bar stages to dive bar stages. And my new friend Brenda hooked me up with Mister Moneybags himself, my future father-in-law, Edward Quartermaine. Well, he wasn't so into it;[273] truth is he wouldn't know entertainment if it put him in stitches. But it wasn't a total loss, because it was when he laughed us off, that Bren came up with the brilliant idea that changed both our lives."

"Edward told Lois she needed to think bigger," says Brenda. "And he was right. She was wasting her talent focusing on one band. She knew all the ins and outs of the music business. Why let record companies call all the shots and hog all the profits?[274] She needed to start her own label."

"And partner with her, of course," says Lois.

And so L&B was born. Brenda and Lois parlayed their success with Eddie Maine and the Idle Rich into developing full-blown

---

[266] L&B was hatched at the Quartermaine estate property and later nurtured at its gatehouse. Its original studio was located at 1111 Ocean Avenue. A state-of-the-art studio was later opened for the revamped label at 550 Grayson Street, Studio Lot J-3.

[267] Lucy's note: "I always knew cosmetics was a cutthroat business—but I had no idea it might result in cut throats! Sonny Corinthos's childhood sponsor, mob boss Joe Scully, was sabotaging my hard-won success at the behest of Damian Smith and Katherine Bell! Those jealous so-and-sos wanted revenge because I'd bested them at their own games! Well the joke was on Scully, because when Sonny learned his former 'benefactor' was getting between good hardworking Port Charlesers and their God-given access to beauty (also there was the teeny tiny matter of Scully planning to rub him out), Sonny shot first! Lucky for Scully, Deception Cosmetics looks as good on the dead as it does on the living. I hear the words on most lips at a mob wake are, 'Who did him in?' At Scully's, all anyone wanted to know was, 'Who did his work?'"

[268] Lucy's note: "Love you, too, Brenda!"

[269] Says Scott B, "Says the former teen princess of plots! If my daughter Karen were alive today, she'd be rolling over in her grave."

[270] Says Brenda's sister, Julia B, "Because I encouraged her to go to college and get a degree? Or perhaps because I sold Deception out from under her, and her modeling job went the way of the popcorn shirt? Either way, she's a better person because she expanded her horizons, and I'll gladly take credit for that."

[271] Says Lois C, "That's an exaggeration."

[272] Says Ned Q, "No it isn't, and my back still bears the scars to prove it."

[273] Says Ned N, "Grandfather was less than into it when he learned Lois's headliner 'Eddie Maine' was me. To him, ELQ and L&B did not mix."

[274] Says Tracy Q, "Why not, indeed! Because what the music industry really needed was another micromanaging control freak."

superstars[275] and award-winning niche acts.[276] The good times wouldn't last forever.[277] Today L&B is more like an indie studio than the industry disruptor it started out as, and Brenda and Lois are both focusing on other endeavors. But one good act is all it takes to spark a comeback, and I hear Lois's daughter[278] can[279] sing . . .[280]

[275] Lucy's note, "And developing sexual chemistry! At one time Brenda was so hot and heavy with up-and-coming heartthrob Miguel Morez that boarding house buttinsky Ruby Anderson threatened to throw them out if their headboard couldn't learn discretion."

[276] Editor's note: Jazz singer Mary Mae Ward.

[277] Editor's note: At times L&B was both a weapon and a casualty of war amongst the Quartermaine family as they fought each other for control of ELQ.

[278] Hurls Lulu S-F, "Ugh, don't get me started."

[279] Unable to help herself, Lulu adds, "My own cousin Carly was after Dante and me, so she pimped out broke-ass Brook Lynn to break us up! As IF oversized hoop earrings, greasy hair, and bargain-basement vocals could turn his head. Carly seriously overplayed her hand and Brook Lynn was relegated to sniffing around for handouts from my brother, Nikolas. Nowadays Dante and I are stronger than ever and Brook Lynn is tearing up the karaoke circuit. You have to wonder why Carly bothered."

[280] Says Michael C in response, "Maybe it had something to do with you and Dante sending me to prison for 'murder' when I was sixteen years old for defending my mother and baby sister from a deranged mob princess? Something like that?"

THE QUARTERMAINE MANSION[281]

My brother Michael has my stepfather Sonny's last name, but he's actually a Quartermaine[282] on his father's side. We try to avoid the subject at home,[283] especially around my mother and Sonny. Mention A.J.'s name and the next thing you're likely to hear is the sound of shattering[284] glassware. So for the sake of bare feet we try never to mention the Q-word—unless you drop it alongside the name Lila.

There's not a person in Port Charles who has an unkind word for Lila[285]—and believe me, I tried to find one. I asked Sonny about her. "Lila was the kindest, most generous person I ever knew," he tells me. "But not naïve. She wasn't blind to a person's faults;[286] but she believed in forgiveness; that people were basically good; give 'em the chance and

they'll learn from their mistakes and grow. It's on account of Lila that Monica's kept up the tradition of opening up her house to people going through hard times[287] who[288] needed support." Brenda had a bunch of stints staying with the Quartermaines, and even once tried to get married there.[289] "She's been in and out so many times we finally decided to dedicate a room just for her inevitable drop-ins," says Mayor Ned Quartermaine. "Every now and then she'll send a shipment of clothes with which to stock the closet."

"Luxury means never carrying a carry-on," Brenda counsels me. Part of me is surprised she doesn't book the penthouse suite at the Metro Court.[290] But I guess even a trust fund baby and famous supermodel sometimes needs family to come home to.

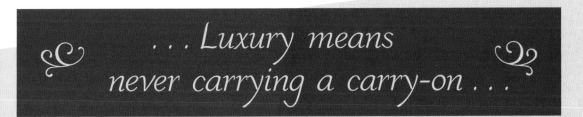

. . . Luxury means never carrying a carry-on . . .

---

[281] 66 Harbor View Road

[282] Editor's note: Michael Corinthos's biological father, A. J. Quartermaine, was murdered in the offices of *Crimson Magazine* in 2014.

[283] Adds Joss, "The list of subjects to avoid at home is actually very long. If you ever find yourself invited over for dinner, make it a point never to reference panic rooms, the Pine Barrens, ax handles, meat hooks, or multiple personalities. Don't ask Sonny about his early days in Port Charles; don't ask my mother about *her* early days in Port Charles; don't ask my grandmother Bobbie about her early days, period. Don't show polite curiosity with my brother Michael about his love life, refrain from asking my stepbrother Dante whether he's ever been hurt in the line of duty, and above all, no matter what else you may do or say, never, ever complain that the coffee in Port Charles is not strong enough.

[284] Say Carly C, "There are worse ways for Sonny to exorcise his frustration by throwing a tumbler or two."

[285] Lucy's note, "She'll always be 'Mother Quartermaine' to me."

[286] Wonders Monica Q, "Perhaps her oft-banished daughter Tracy would care to offer comment?"

[287] Editor's note: At one time or another the Quartermaine estate has been home to Monica's friend and cancer sufferer Paige Bowen; Paige's daughter, Emily, adopted by Alan and Monica after Paige's death; Karen Wexler; an assortment of former Quartermaine spouses; and the occasional fake Quartermaine heir—like Kiki Jerome, once thought to be the daughter of artist-turned-serial killer-turned-art therapist Franco, once thought to be Jason Morgan's twin.

[288] Says Tracy Q, "Also strays, hangers-on, and parasites."

[289] Says Sonny C, "Did I go to the Philippines and dredge up Jax's presumed dead wife, Miranda? Yes. Did I bring Miranda back to Port Charles and escort her to Jax and Brenda's wedding? Yes I did. Was I invited? No—but I have never been one to stand on ceremony. Better to cause some heartache in the short-term to avoid a lifetime of misery."

[290] Says Carly C, "As half-owner of the Metro Court Hotel, I make sure we're always booked when Brenda barrels into town."

ST. TIMOTHY'S CHURCH[291]

When you step into the peaceful manicured gardens of St. Timothy's, the first thing you hear is nothing at all. The hubbub of North Main goes poof, sopped up by the high, sharp hedgerows and brick walls that provide sanctuary for the spiritual from the swamped. The first thing you notice is the glow the light lends to the stonework of the church, as though it's been carved right out of the cliffs of Dover.

Then your hearing adjusts and you take in the call of birdsong and the tinkle of a four-tiered fountain. The church doors are flung open to welcome all, and through them you can see the altar, painted in colors spilling through the stained glass windows inside. It's no wonder Brenda chose this magical place to marry Sonny;[292] and then again as the place to meet him a few years later,[293] when she returned to Port Charles. Which makes it even more appalling that he got gunned down there.[294] St. Timothy's is a more peaceful place these days.[295] But if you visit, do yourself a favor: don't ask Father where Sonny Corinthos got shot.

[291] 1123 North Main Street

[292] Says J Jacks, "Except he *didn't* marry her. She waited for him as the heavens opened, but he never came. He left her there, standing in the rain."

[293] Says Brenda, "Everyone thought I died after my very ill mother drove us off a cliff into the ocean. I survived and was nursed back to health by a bad dude—arms dealer Luis Alcazar—who wanted to keep me in his gilded cage. After years with him, I finally escaped and took off running for the one person I knew I could trust . . ."

[294] Says Sonny C, "Except Jason and I saw it coming, so we were ready with the fake out. If I'd known it was Brenda waiting to meet me—and not one of Alcazar's hit men—I'd have done things differently. But what're ya gonna do, right?"

[295] Editor's note: Church gossip suggests that after his non-shooting, Sonny gave a generous contribution to the Feast of San Gennaro, as well as a promise to give confession elsewhere.

Weighing in with an appreciation for all that Port Charles's burgeoning media industry has to offer is *Crimson Magazine*'s executive fashion editor, Maxie Jones-West. Royal Daughter of Port Charles's Prince of Pop[296] and only Aztec princess,[297] few are as uniquely qualified[298] as Maxie to guide us through the ins and outs of our city's tastemakers as the two-time honoree of the Port Charles Press's Award for "Best Dressed at A Ball, Wedding, or Natural Disaster."

[296] Editor's note: One-man Buzzfeed hairstyle slideshow Frisco Jones.
[297] Editor's note: She of the Betty Boop voice and Rapunzel tresses, Felicia Scorpio, née Cummings.
[298] Says Nina R, "What am I, yesterday's shoulder pads?"

MATTERS

Technically, the offices of *Crimson Magazine* are not open to the public. How can we be expected to churn out two hundred glossy pages of scintillating fashion news and commentary every month only to stop the presses every time an outsider barges in for a peek into the famous *Crimson* closet! But! Catch us on the right day[300] and we may be in just the mood[301] to give you an insider's look at how the sausage is made—and how many chinchillas died to make it.[302] The first maven of the masthead was Kate[303] Howard.[304] She was in the market for a new opportunity after being unceremoniously ousted from her role as editor[305] of the industry leader, *Couture* magazine. Thankfully, angel investor Jasper Jacks stepped in with a cash infusion that Kate used to found the upstart *Crimson*. *Crimson* totally disrupted the rag trade for a while—until Kate's past[306] caught up with her.[307] Eventually she got better and was even settling down with her childhood sweetheart, Sonny,[308] when tragedy struck: she was shot and killed[309] in her own office! My hero was gone.[310] *Crimson* might have gone the way of the drop[311] crotch[312] had Julian Jerome[313] not hired Nina Reeves.[314] Nina

[299] Corporate HQ located in the office block at the Metro Court Hotel, 1420 Quartz Lane, Suite 301.

[300] Says *Crimson* editor in chief Nina Reeves, "After we've met deadline."

[301] Says *Crimson* editor in chief Nina Reeves, "Drunk."

[302] Says *Crimson* editor in chief Nina Reeves, "She's kidding, people! We neither eat nor wear chinchillas at *Crimson*! We are a fur-free periodical!" Adds Maxie, "Except for the fur that flies at budget meetings."

[303] Snorts Carly C, "*Not* her real name. When 'Kate Howard' stepped off the train to start her freshman year in Princeton, she left Connie Falconeri from Bensonhurt behind. I guess she decided all those vowels didn't fit the new her."

[304] Says Sonny C, "It was more complicated than that and Carly knows it. Some bad stuff had happened to Connie back in Brooklyn—bad enough to give her a toxic case of D.I.D. [Editor's note: dissociative identity disorder]. 'Kate Howard' was a new personality, one that didn't carry all of Connie's baggage. Be nice, Carly."

[305] Says Ric L, "My father pined for Kate [Editor's note: Ric's father was attorney/mob boss Trevor Lansing, onetime head of the Zacchara crime family]. She in turn pined for my half brother Sonny—because who doesn't? Trevor exploited Kate's commitment to her career in an effort to drive a wedge between her and Sonny. He called in some favors and saw to it advertisers pulled their spreads from *Couture*, hoping to extort Kate into making a break with Sonny. Kate dug in her heels [says Maxie, "Ankle straps, sling backs, corsets, or commas, Connie/Kate rocked them all."] but was eventually fired for breach of contract tied to an arrest and conviction for reckless driving."

[306] Editor's note: In the form of a childhood tormentor, Joe Scully Jr.

[307] Says Carly C, "Her D.I.D. went full-on TNT. Kate became Connie, destroyer of birthday cakes."

[308] Says Kate/Connie's cousin Olivia F-Q, "We were both his childhood sweethearts, mmkay?"

[309] Says Carly C, "By Ava Jerome, of the Ava Jerome Gallery and helium heels. Just in case anyone forget what she's capable of since the justice system around here seems to have a very short memory."

[310] Adds Maxie, "Though there are times when I still feel her presence. Usually when I arrive at the office in the morning with misgivings about a particular outfit. It's almost as though I can hear her wag and wonder, 'Those shoes with that belt? Did I teach you nothing?'"

[311] Editor's note: Technically not yet gone.

[312] Says Nina R, "Please Dear God let it be soon."

[313] Editor's note: Julian Jerome—then masquerading under the alias Derek Wells—bought *Crimson Magazine* and its parent company in 2013, adding it to his portfolio at Derek Wells Media.

[314] Says Nina R, "To drive it into the ground! That rat bastard took me for a moron, thought I'd tank *Crimson* so hard he could close it down and make a mint on the tax write-off. Well I showed him! Today I'm Boss Bitch and he's slinging mozzarella sticks at Charlie's Pub!

employed new and adventurous means[315] of marketing[316] the magazine, ultimately lifting circulation and putting it back in the black. *Crimson* remains an industry vanguard and is growing by leaps and bounds, bucking the industry trend. So if you're new to Port Charles and looking to break into publishing, drop in the day after deadline, and bring a résumé.[317] Tell 'em Cartullo sent you.

[315] Says Nina, "Like air-dropping thousands of *Crimson* pages all over major cities! Whoever pieced together and delivered an entire issue won big-time!"

[316] Says PCPD Detective Dante Falconeri, "Also known as mass littering, or dumping; in this case an arrestable offense."

[317] Maxie offers this helpful hint: We might be better primed to catch a whiff of your CV if it's spritzed with a dash of Deception perfume—but not Enchantment. Nina loathes Enchantment.

THE PORT CHARLES PRESS[318]

The *Port Charles Press*[319] is our hometown answer to the *New York Times*. The *Press* breaks lots of stories,[320] but it also breaks lives. Whoever is in charge over there[321] seriously needs to replace their HR department[322] and ombudsman and get a firm handle on its ethics. There's investigative journalism and there's exploitation. I'd say that it's only a matter of time before the *Press* gets someone killed: BUT OH WAIT.[323]

AURORA MEDIA

In the fall of 2017, my dear friend Sam and her husband,[324] Drew, decided to make a clean break from the life of violence and retribution that was part and parcel of his work enforcing the will of Sonny Corinthos.[325] So they pooled their resources and bought up her old man Julian's[326] business, Derek Wells Media. Aurora owns a wide variety of concerns, including old media (*Crimson Magazine*, the *Port Charles Press*) and new (the popular Web browser Spyder Finder).

WXPC[327]

Our most notable local television station,[328] WXPC, is famous for its breaking news coverage, human-interest pieces, and the long tenure of anchor Tiffany Hill.[329] In addition to its reporting,

---

[318] 245 East Main Street

[319] Originally the *Port Charles Herald*; during Llanview, PA, transplant Todd Manning's brief reign, it was re-branded the *Port Charles Sun*.

[320] Says Lulu F, "I cover everything from school cafeteria graft to the capture of international terrorists like Cesar Faison."

[321] Editor's note: Please see the next section.

[322] Agrees Anna D, "For heaven's sake, they once hired Heather Webber to run their gossip column!"

[323] Says Lulu F, "I take full responsibility for the events of early 2018 that led to the death of Detective James Nathan West. I published a series of articles, including an interview with Detective West designed to lure from hiding his father, Cesar Faison. Faison took the bait. But I did not anticipate the chain reaction that would then unfold, resulting in Detective West's shooting death by his own father. Detective West left behind a pregnant wife, my best friend, Maxie Jones-West. Maxie, if it is any consolation, I wish it had been me." Responds Maxie, "It isn't."

[324] Editor's note: At the time of the events described, Sam's husband was legally Jason Morgan. However, it was soon revealed that the real Jason Morgan had been held in a drugged sleep for the preceding five years. The man to whom Sam was married was in actuality Jason's twin brother, Drew, who had been kidnapped at birth and as an adult subjected to an experimental therapy that effectively replaced his own memories with that of his twin brother's. Drew believed he was Jason; until the real Jason busted through a skylight to halt a hostage-taking at the party announcing the creation of Aurora Media.

[325] Says Corinthos lawyer Diane Miller, "Sonny is a simple purveyor of fine Colombian coffee beans. Get them at any Perks location or wherever quality coffee is found."

[326] Says Alexis D, "Julian was undergoing some legal issues at the time. Come to think of it, that phrase is applicable to any period of his adult life."

[327] 4225 Liberty Avenue

[328] Editor's note: Re-branded from the original WLPC.

[329] Tiffany Hill, star of such B movies as *Death Church, Death Church II: Holy Sea of Blood*, and *Death Church IV: I Am the Resurrection and the Knife*. (Editor's note: Hill chose not to return for *Death Church III: Diocese of the Damned*. Her part was played by Megan Gordon, who later went on to star as twins Roxanne and Ruby Bright in the network television soap opera *Fraternity Row*.

WXPC has produced such original fare as daytime talk shows *Everyday*[330] *Heroes*[331] and *The Colton Connection.*[332]

THE *INVADER*[333]

We've got our *New York Times*, and we also have our New York Post—the tabloid *Invader*. Sleazy Mel Mason edits this fish wrap, which has a great gossip page[334] and a reputation for foul odor,[335] but not much else.

Some people visit Port Charles with amour on the mind. And who can blame them? This city is lousy with love—although some of its inhabitants are just plain lousy with it. We Port Charlesers are an idealistic lot—one crash and burn is not going to turn us off from passion and commitment. Heck, two, three, four crash and burns won't do it, either! If you look to find your other half in Port Charles, the odds are in your favor. We enjoy a marriage rate double the national average![336] And that doesn't include drunken elopements to Las Vegas![337] Get ready to receive a romance of your own by taking one of these tours specially designed to follow in the footsteps of some of our most famous couples. You too may discover that truer love was never forged than love made in Port Charles. . . .

> *. . . the Invader has a great gossip page . . .*

---

[330] Says producer Amelia Joffe, "I was developing a talk show about regular citizens doing the impossible. The concept was perfect for its time; *Oprah* was still on, everyone wanted something aspirational. It was an easy sell. All I needed was the right host. I found her when I tuned in to live coverage of the Metro Court Hotel hostage crisis of 2007. A lone hostage escaped, shimmying out from behind the giant hotel sign over the entrance, jumping to the ground and pulling off her mask. It was a beautiful, ballsy brunette. She ran over to the police cordon and warned them that the hostage takers inside had wired the lobby to blow. The police prepared to take action but then everything went to hell. I never forgot about that woman. She was the epitome of the "everyday hero" I wanted to feature. So, I sought her out and made her my host.

[331] Says Sam M, "Hiring me probably had more to do with her wanting to get revenge on me for killing her father—which, okay, yes, I did kill him, but it was in self-defense."

[332] Says Lucy, "My cousin Colton briefly hosted a talk show where he explored inspiring stories and gave advice." Reached for comment, Colton had this to say: "It was fun while it lasted, but my days of advice were over once it came out I'd once been brainwashed by international terrorist Nicholas "Domino" Van Buren to assassinate Frisco Jones and God knows who else."

[333] 1211 Seneca Street

[334] Memorable headlines include, "WXPC to Replace Tiffany Over-the-Hill—with Talking Hamster?!"; "Quartermaine Quandary! Monica Q Noodles with Edward's Ghost! Madame Maia Tells All!"; "Jackie 'Wacky Tobacky' Templeton Back to Rehab—This Time It's Pork Rinds!"

[335] Says Lulu F, "Maxie and I once got arrested for setting off a stink bomb in their offices and posing as the EPA in order to get a look at their books and find out who sold them the story of the real identity behind the advice-for-bros book *Ask Man Landers* (news flash . . . it wasn't a man). I remember that caper fondly." Says her husband, Detective Dante Falconeri, "We still get complaints about the reek in the holding cells."

[336] Says attorney Scott B, "The divorce rate is even higher. Call me at 716-555-ENDS when it's finally costing you more to stay together than it is to part ways.

[337] Including but not limited to such betrothals as Luke Spencer to Tracy Quartermaine, Scott Baldwin to Dominique Stanton, Hayden Barnes and Nikolas Cassadine, and Trey Mitchell to Kristina Corinthos.

SONNY AND CARLY

One of the things people are most curious about when they learn I live in Port Charles is Sonny Corinthos.[338] "What's he really like?" they ask me. "Does he carry a gun? Has he ever shot you? He's not actually that handsome in real life, is he?" To which I answer, "A more cuddlesome Tony Soprano," "at least one in each pocket," "no, but not for lack of desire, I'm sure," and "For sure, but he's so not my type." He is, however, wife Carly's type on the woman most often his mate,[339] Carly. And the best person to lead you on this tour of the torrid is none other than the Alfred to Sonny's Batman, his longtime driver and bodyguard, Max Giambetti:

History is littered with star-crossed lovers: Frankie and Johnny, Guinevere and Lancelot, the dish and the spoon. Here in Port Charles, we have my boss, Sonny Corinthos, and the former, now current, Mrs. C. Grab a cup of coffee, queue up some Sinatra, and come take a stroll with me through some of their most memorable moments. . . .

---

[338] For the full skinny on his crimes and misdemeanors, visit "The Museum of Mayhem" for the "Sonny Corinthos Virtual Reality Experience" package.

[339] Editor's note: Sonny has been romantically linked to student-turned-stripper-turned-doctor Karen Wexler, supermodel snitch Brenda Barrett, car-bombed Lily Rivera, Sam McCall (whom his right-hand man would snap up), orphan Emily Quartermaine, Brooklyn-babe Connie Falconeri (and her split personality ice queen Kate Howard), lady mobster Claudia Zacchara, and lady mobster part two Ava Jerome, to name but a few.

122 HARBOR VIEW DRIVE, PH-4

Sonny doesn't live here anymore, but he still owns the place. Check out the listing on Airbnb. It doesn't come cheap but the views are worth the cost—and so's the history. This place is full of it, including the incident in question. It took place before my employment with Mr. C began, but I gathered the deets for you because it's the Big One, the thing that finally got Mr. C to start recasting the love of his life from Brenda Barrett. The way I hear it went down is like this: Mrs. C—before she was Mrs. C—had it real bad for Jason. But one day she sees him slow dancing[340] with Elizabeth Webber at Kelly's[341] and then took off for Sonny's penthouse. Whenever I ask Mrs. C why she went looking for him[342] in the first place, she never has an answer.[343] Maybe it's because she knew that's where their love story began. Sonny was home and they fought, he said some things that weren't nice, she said some things that were equally not nice, and suddenly that thin line between love and hate vanished because it was right then and there that they first did the horizontal mambo.[344]

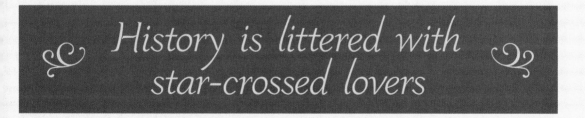

History is littered with star-crossed lovers

[340] Says Liz W, "I was in a horrible mood after a teacher rendered a hurtful critique of a piece that was very important to me. Jason comforted me, that's all."

[341] Opines Max, "Dancing of any sort is my ideal way to spend the afternoon if you ask me, a certain lawyer (and I always take a moment in the day to cut a rug).

[342] Asks Olivia F-Q, "Are you kidding? Have you seen that face?"

[343] Asks Sonny C, "Why are you asking her at all?!"

[344] Says Sonny C, "Max, you and I are going to have a stern talk about boundaries."

PORT CHARLES COURTHOUSE[345]

This place has a lot of bad associations for the boss and Mrs. C, so you may think it strange it's also the site of my favorite of their nuptials (their third of four).[346] It's nice when flower arrangements eclipse federal arraignments, if you know what I mean. The boss was on the hook for shooting one of his enemies,[347] and Mrs. C had seen it happen. No way was she gonna avoid having to testify against the father of her sons. But Sonny's foxy lawyer, Diane Miller,[348] played matchmaker and soon enough Sonny and Carly were saying their "I-dos" in court. Some might say that the marriage was one of convenience—but nobody who knows them buys that, because since when have those two ever made anything convenient for any of us? Mrs. C was "in love" with Jax at the time and went to great lengths to remind Sonny that their marriage would be a legal transaction, nothing more. Imagine Mrs. C's face when Mr. C produced a real ring for the "fake" ceremony. Something she never knew: he actually had her ring made by a jeweler in Martinique, where they first really feel in love. Now is that some *Casablanca*-level romance or what?

PORT CHARLES CEMETERY[349]

You know that moment in *Tom Sawyer* where he and Huck go to their own funeral and get to listen to everybody cry their eyes out over their loss? Well this is like that but different. We all thought Mrs. C had died in a car crash after getting an eyeful[350] back home. But she survived and walked into the church to find everybody mourning her death. She didn't take too kindly to the sight of a casket meant to hold her body and took off. Mr. C gave chase and caught up to her in the cemetery where she was understandably discomposed. But Mr. C is nothing if not her anchor. He took her hand and told her she was home. And she was. Home is anywhere, so long as it's with him.

> *It's nice when flower arrangements eclipse federal arraignments . . .*

---

[345] 1442 Central Avenue

[346] Lucy's note: Are we counting the renewal of wedding vows?

[347] Says Corinthos lawyer Diane Miller, "Lorenzo Alcazar, in an act of self-defense!"

[348] Says Corinthos family lawyer Diane Miller, "That is speculation entirely unsupported by established fact, and I move it stricken from the record!"

[349] 1123 North Main Street

[350] Sighs Alexis D, "No need to be coy, Max. Everyone knows the eyeful was Sonny and me in bed together."

PENTONVILLE PRISON[351]

A visit to Pentonville Prison probably does not appear on many tours, but in addition to its impressive brutalist architecture and a very finely woven barbed wire fence, this is also the place Mr. and Mrs. C finally arrived at some very important truths. Nothing like enduring a full-body pat down and cavity search to prove how much you care. Mr. C had been sentenced to prison.[352] Like so many romantic heroes before him, he abides by that age-old adage that if you love something, like a red balloon or a 1952 Topps Mickey Mantle baseball card, you gotta let it go. When Mrs. C came to see him at Pentonville, he told her to let him go and move on with her life with someone else. "I love you," he told her. "Don't look back." Carly's been looking back ever since.

351 Editor's note: Located at 628 Fairfax Road, Pentonville, NY. Buses run twice daily from the Port Charles police station. You could also get there by committing a violent felony; but conviction rates in Port Charles are notoriously low.
352 Says Monica Q, "For murdering my son, A.J. Just so there's no confusion."

LULU AND DANTE

Sonny isn't the only Corinthos with a relish for romance. His first-born, Detective Dante Falconeri, is known to have set many hearts aflame, but he burns for just one woman: Lulu Spencer. Here's the person who knows him second best to give a tour of their love, Dante's mother, the first lady of Port Charles, Olivia Falconeri-Quartermaine.

I never lie about my kids.[353] The God's honest truth is that my Dante is the biggest thing since my ancestors stomped their first grape. I worried my whole life that he'd never meet a woman half as good as he is. But I worried in vain. Dante met his match in the form of Port Charles's Lulu Spencer. Grab a cannoli and walk in the footsteps of these two knuckleheads' greatest hits.

❧ I never lie about my kids ❧

---

[353] Adds Olivia, "Except when his life depends on it."

JAKE'S BAR[354]

Growing up, my Uncle Tony always used to say, *"Il bar non porta i ricordi. Sono i ricordi che portano al bar."* I'm told this roughly translates to, "Drink up, the bar doesn't bring memories. Memories bring you to the bar." It makes sense that my boy would meet the love of his life at this dive turned rib joint.

It was here in 2009 that Dante and Lulu got friendly and flirtatious over a game of pool—which then led to her hooligan[355] brothers beating the snot out of my poor son.[356] Lulu saw past Dante's bravado and their love story began. . . .

---

[354] Located at 345 Portside Road. In 2012, Jake's was rechristened The Floating Rib as an homage to a long-shuttered Port Charles culinary institution, and also to remove painful connotations to Elizabeth Webber's then-presumed dead son, Jake.

[355] Argues Ethan L, "I am nobody's hooligan. A ruffian, maybe. A rogue, definitely."

[356] Laments Lucky S, "I thought he was one of Sonny's soldiers! I couldn't have him nosing around my baby sister! If I'd known he was an undercover cop, I would not have broken a pool cue on his arm."

THE HAUNTED STAR NIGHTCLUB AND CASINO[357]

Right after their meeting Dante and Lulu ran into each other again at a favorite spot for arguments and affairs—and everything that falls in between. When I heard about this encounter, I was reminded of a similar tactic he drew on with Donna Martucci[358] at the playground back home in Bensonhurst. Dante dared Lulu to kiss him. Of course, no one can turn on the charm like my kid when he wants to, and Lulu—being a Spencer—is not one to turn down a dare. As another one of my favorite family sayings goes, "The kiss is to love as lightning is to thunder."

ABANDONED ZACCHARA PROPERTY (N/A)[359]

While searching an old Zacchara crime family property for Carly and her kidnapper,[360] Lulu fell through the decaying floorboards and into some freezing water below. Dante jumped in with Lulu to keep her warm while waiting for help to arrive. And while they nearly froze to death manufacturing their take on a happier ending to *Titanic*, Dante revealed to her that he was actually an undercover cop tasked with getting the goods on Sonny . . . which he would do—right before Sonny shot him. His own father![361]

682 PAULSON STREET #4-B

As you may have noticed, my family has a saying for every occasion. From Uncle Tony comes this gem, *"Non tutte le ciambelle riescono col buco."* ("Not all doughnuts come out with a hole.") Put another way, things don't always turn out as planned. Lulu was at sixes and sevens after finding out about some infidelity in her family.[362] She came tearing over to Dante's apartment looking for some assurance that their relationship wasn't part of his cover, to which Dante responded with words I know for a fact he never told another girl: "I love you." Dante didn't mean to fall in love when he came to Port Charles, and he didn't mean for Port Charles to become his home, but what happened when he and Lulu met brings the old Italian saying to life: *Chi si volta, e chi si gira, sempre a casa va finire.* "If you're with your love, no matter where you go or turn, you'll always end up at home." Kinda like another Italian guy I know, name of Corinthos. . . .

---

[357] 100 Commodore Way, Pier 23

[358] Says Olivia, "A lovely girl who went to dental school and is now a hygienist in Bay Ridge. Criminally single. If it hadn't been Lulu, I'd have made sure Dante wound up back in Donna's orbit."

[359] Says Olivia, "I'm not giving up this location because the last thing anybody needs is a bunch of impressionable kids hanging around dilapidated old houses trying to re-create a death-defying moment. Just read the description and imagine it!"

[360] Lucy's note, "Loony tunes mob heiress Claudia Zacchara."

[361] Says Corinthos family lawyer Diane Miller, "Sonny was never convicted of such a crime. Detective Falconeri reported that the shooting was an accident of his own making. Sonny, I do hope you know I'm charging my regular rate for this fact-checking."

[362] Says Sam M, "Liz was with one of Lulu's brothers and cheating on him with another of Lulu's brothers. Go big or go home, that's what Liz says."

FRISCO AND FELICIA

People feel so strongly about our town, they're coming out of retirement to welcome you! Sean Donely[363] volunteered to write up his assessment of one of Port Charles's greatest loves of all, his old pals in adventuring: Frisco Jones[364] and Felicia Jones Scorpio.

I've never known two people more right for each other and worse at making it last than Frisco and Felicia. What they've been through together—and trying to be together—could fill a book all on its own. Think Shakespeare romance by way of *It Happened One Night*. I've boiled their story down to a short stroll by spots that always conjure my fondest memories of these two, starting right on the corner of bitter and sweet.

> *I've never known two people more right for each other . . .*

---

[363] Former PCPD commissioner and ex-WSB agent Sean Donely currently resides in Ireland with wife, Tiffany Hill, star of such B movies as *The Stiffening*, *The Tightening*, and *Samson & Delilah 2: Locks of Love*.
[364] Lucy's note, "My former brother-in-law."

900 NORTH YALE PLACE

Frisco and the Riff Raff's 1984 charity concert at the Avalon Spa was cut short by a police action . . . but his night was far from over. He quickly conked out upon retiring to his apartment on North Yale—unaware that he wasn't alone in his room. Hiding beneath his bed was the spritely valet who had helped unload his band's equipment just hours ago. Frisco caught the kid red-handed trying to steal his ring right off the nightstand. "For a long time, the kid didn't say a word," Frisco reminisces. "I offered coffee. I threatened to call the cops. I didn't get what the big deal was. The ring couldn't have been worth more than twenty bucks. Finally the kid makes a break for it and in the commotion I tear his

hat off and lo and behold he is a she." "All I wanted was my grandmother's ring," says Felicia. "It was a family heirloom—Aztec."

Felicia revealed to him that she was descended from Aztec royalty and that she herself was a princess. Her family's heritage was bound up in an ancient treasure that had been looted, and she was only trying to get it back from the marauders. Thus began a tortured saga of two crazy kids in an apartment that rarely managed hot water. From that night forward, Frisco made sure that old hat of Felicia's[365] was never far from his grasp. I like to think it helped remind him sometimes the best things are hidden in plain sight.

1242 ELM DRIVE

The next stop on your tour du Jones is located in the historic Brownstone District. Here you'll find the town house owned by Frisco and Felicia's pal, Bobbie Spencer. After their madcap search for the Aztec treasure finally concluded,[366] they decided to move in together. I used to call their studio apartment at Bobbie's[367] "The Dump," and that was being generous. The water was brown and the walls were paper-thin, but it didn't matter to Frisco and Felicia. Their happiness was contagious, and all-consuming. Soon wedding bells were in the air, but their plans to do

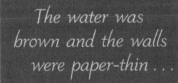

The water was brown and the walls were paper-thin . . .

it up in grand style went out the window when Felicia tried to call the whole thing off. "I'm just not cut out to be a policeman's wife," she moaned.[368] Felicia managed to pull it together for a ceremony and reception in the backyard of the brownstone. I'll never forget the minister Bobbie practically abducted off a tennis court to marry them that day. I was tasked with giving Felicia away, and it's a moment I've always regretted. Nobody "gives" Felicia away. She gives of herself, by her own will and by her own choice.

---

[365] Says Sean, "She'll always be Princess to me."

[366] Supplies Sean, "In the interest of transparency, the hunt ended with my apprehension. I'd been after the treasure for a long time. In the end, it went back to its rightful owners and Princess and I let bygones be bygones and became great friends.

[367] Says Bobbie S, "This coming from a man who went by the nickname "El Patrón" and perpetrated no end of shady deals in the so-called name of the WSB. I freely admit the brownstone has been a fixer-upper from time to time; but so, Sean, have you."

[368] Suggests Sean, "I wish I'd told her my hunch that that particular career choice was never going to take, anyway."

PORT CHARLES INTERNATIONAL AIRPORT, DEPARTURE LOUNGE[369]

Bookmark this stop on the tour when you're on your way out of town.[370] This was the scene of one of Port Charles's most tear-jerking goodbyes. After a stint with the PCPD, Frisco felt that old familiar tug known as wanderlust and joined the WSB. A fully fledged agent, Frisco was assigned a mission that would take him out of town for what he was told would only be a short while. Felicia accompanied him to the airport[371] to bid him adieu. In front of a poster promoting Chicago tourism, Frisco bade our Princess a tearful goodbye, promising to return. In fitting style, each gave each other a gift filled with meaning: Felicia gave Frisco a silver-framed wedding picture, to which he responded, "I'll kiss this every morning and every night." Frisco gave Felicia a gold locket[372] containing the inscription, "Lady of My Heart."[373]

THE CATACOMBS

Grab your kit from PC Adventures Outfitter and head underground to seek out Frisco's sanctuary from his deadly pursuers. It was here in 1989 that Frisco spirited Felicia after she fainted from the shock of coming face-to-face with the husband she thought was dead— presumed so the year before, the victim[374] of a WSB mission gone awry.[375] Frisco declared his love once more to a conflicted Felicia— who had not long before married Colton, the very man once believed to have been Frisco's killer.[376] Said Frisco, "We were meant to be together, and I know you believe in that." That line eventually worked, and Felicia reunited with Frisco . . . for a while anyway.

---

[369] 142 Edgar Drive

[370] Lucy's note: But who would ever want to leave?

[371] Editor's note: This was in 1987, that heady time when anyone could walk up to an airport gate regardless of whether or not they held a ticket.

[372] The "Lady My Heart" replica pendent is available at Wyndham's Department Store, located at 620 North Main Street, for $49.95 and is a perfect Valentine's Day gift for the lady you keep coming back to.

[373] Says Frisco J, "She still is."

[374] Says Frisco J, "I'd get into it, but you don't have the WSB clearance."

[375] Says Felicia J, "Fortunately I don't work for those spooks in the WSB, so I don't need clearance. Frisco's operation to expose some international terrorists had succeeded, but they cornered him at the last second and led everyone to believe they'd killed him, when really he was held in a Middle Eastern prison, where no one was allowed a shave or a haircut. Colton was the one who helped me track down Frisco's supposed final resting place in Quebec. He really was a swell guy."

[376] Says Colton S, "Turns out it was really a group of terrorists who 'killed' Frisco, not me. I'd only been brainwashed into thinking I'd done it. Go figure."

1020 NORTH STATE STREET[377]

Robert Scorpio's apartment in LiSy was the first place that Felicia and Frisco played house. Robert left Robin[378] in their care[379] while he[380] searched[381] for answers[382] in New York City. It was amazing watching those two find their rhythm as parents; too bad it didn't take. Thinking of how great Frisco was with Robin, telling her stories and making her pancakes, made me wish Frisco had been around to see her tend to his own girls.[383] But Frisco was always Port Charles's answer to Peter Pan, and Felicia was his Wendy, waiting for him to land after each adventure, until the day she finally had to close the window and he had no place left to land.

[377] 1020 North State Street
[378] Says Robert S, "I didn't then know that Robin was my daughter. Otherwise I wouldn't have left her with those randy kids."
[379] Says Robin S-D, "That's probably why I'm so messed up today."
[380] Says Anna D, "Still can't believe Robert did that."
[381] Says Robert S, "Everybody calm down. Robin's just joking."
[382] Asks Carly C, "*Is* she, though?"
[383] Comments Maxie J-W, "Yeah, that might have been nice."

LUKE AND LAURA

Our next tour guide needs no introduction save this: Here's former teenaged hooker Bobbie Spencer! You can choose your friends, but you can't choose your family. I confess here and now that there have been times I wished I could! Being the kid sister to the infamous Luke Spencer can be exhausting. But over the years it's also afforded me a front-row seat to one of Port Charles's greatest love stories. The tale of Luke and Laura and their thrilling adventures brought massive attention to our city. Heck, they even once landed on the cover of *Newsweek*!

I wouldn't be surprised if the reason we get most of our visitors is because of the stories you've heard about them. Well, follow me, and we'll hit all the highs—and maybe some of the lows. Why am I the best qualified to give this tour, you wonder? Well who else knows all their secrets but me?

> *. . . the reason we get most of our visitors is because of the stories you've heard about them*

THE WEBBER HOUSE[384]

Our tour begins at this gorgeous 1912 gable front home. Though it had many owners, the most prominent was Dr. Lesley Williams.[385] You could say that Lesley was a pioneer for her time. In the era when women were marching in the streets for equality, Lesley was fighting her own battle against the status quo at medical school. She came to Port Charles in the early seventies as a prominent cardiologist. Lesley was stunned to learn that not far away there lived Laura Vining—a teenaged girl whom Lesley had given up for adoption as a baby!

Lesley sought out Laura and forged a mother/daughter bond that eventually had Laura move in with Lesley and her new husband, Dr. Rick Webber.[386] Their new picture-perfect family didn't last long, as Rick's college roommate David Hamilton moved in with the family for a while. David seduced teenage Laura, ending her relationship with Scotty Baldwin . . . though I, then a fresh-faced nurse, was more than happy to keep Scotty company.

> . . . I . . . was more than happy to keep Scotty company

But all was not as it seemed! David was using Laura in an ill-conceived attempt to make Lesley jealous. When Laura discovered the truth, she snapped and accidentally pushed David to his death. The act of desperation sent Laura back into Scotty's arms. Laura was convicted of voluntarily manslaughter and sentenced to probation—somehow not the relief to her that it would've been to just about anyone else—and given a mandatory curfew until she became a legal adult. Scott and Laura realized there was a loophole to the court's ruling; they could get married. They soon did—a turn of events that turned my stomach and hardened my heart.

THE CAMPUS DISCO[387]

When one thinks of the 1970s, one thinks of Halston, auteurs, gas shortages. But if one has any sense at all, one mostly thinks of disco! The hustle, the bump and the electric slide were all the craze at PCU, and if you had a tail feather to shake, it got shook at the Campus Disco—a haven of dancing, drinks, and dining for folks young and young at heart.[388] My torch for Scotty was still burning hot like a disco inferno and I was determined to end his relationship with Laura. So I decided to call in a favor from my roguish brother, Luke.

---

[384] 41 Aconbury Way

[385] Says Monica Q: "Lesley was dubbed 'The Widow Faulkner' after the suspicious death of her first husband. Me? I just called her 'Lester.'"

[386] Editor's note: Monica Quartermaine vehemently disputes Rick Webber's role in another that occurred in this home's attic in 2002. It should be noted that Dr. Quartermaine came to believe this while under the influence of a non-FDA–approved relish.

[387] 22 Eastman Lane

[388] Asks Richard S, "What am I, chopped liver? I slimmed bodies and fed self-esteem there for years!"

When my plan to have him break up the happy couple didn't go as I planned, I expected him to head back to Florida. Instead, he stuck around as the disco's manager . . . in addition to running errands for mobster Frank Smith. Laura got a job as a waitress at the disco. It turns out my instincts were correct, as the attraction between the dangerous Luke and ingénue Laura was palpable! Luke's desire for Laura reached a fever pitch on the night Frank Smith ordered him to assassinate a senatorial candidate.[389] When Luke didn't go through with the hit, he became a marked man himself . . .[390]

WYNDHAM'S DEPARTMENT STORE[391]

As Laura was grappling with her feelings for Luke, he was figuring out how to survive Frank Smith's executioners. After stealing Frank Smith's "little black book" of encoded secrets, Luke went to see Laura. They admitted their feelings for one another but knew they would only be safe to pursue those feelings once Frank Smith was brought down. They decided to go on the run together, at least until they could decipher the code in Frank's book, which they hoped would provide the leverage to rid themselves of his threat for good.

Luke and Laura spent their first night on the lam holed up in the august Wyndham's Department Store, where they dressed up and waltzed down deserted aisles full of high-end clothing, jewelry, perfume, and cosmetics.[392] Wyndham's stores may have popped up in every shopping mall throughout the country . . . but its flagship remains right here in Port Charles!

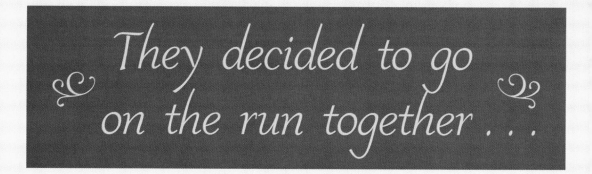

They decided to go on the run together . . .

[389] Editor's note: The characterization here glosses over what ought to have been considered then and would certainly be considered now a criminal act. Though for many years labeled a "seduction," Luke and Laura have both since reckoned with the events of that evening and agree that what took place was the sexual assault of a young woman by an older, powerful man who neither sought nor received consent for his actions. Although a storied couple would later emerge from these events, we would be remiss to whitewash their dark origins. A more frank, in-depth dialogue about this episode in Port Charles history is a highlight of Amelia Joffe's course, "Patriarchal Sway over Local Lore" given at Port Charles University.

[390] Says Jennifer S, "My father offered to let him live if he'd marry me. He chose death. I've tried not to take that personally over the years, but it was when Luke rejected me that I began to eat my feelings."

[391] 620 North Main Street

[392] Lucy: My beloved Coe Co Cosmetics has, alas, folded. But Wyndham's fourth floor features a rare perfumes boutique that carries a limited supply of some of the nation's last stocks of Coe Co products, as well as those of Jacks Cosmetics and the company that started them all, the one, the only Deception! At various times, Deception has been run by Julia Barrett, Dominique Stanton, Scott Baldwin, Carly Corinthos, Laura Spencer herself, and *moi*!

DETOUR

BEECHER'S CORNERS: If you have an extra day during your stay in Port Charles, I suggest a visit to picturesque Beecher's Corners. It's a beautiful farming community a short drive south of the city.[393] Luke and Laura spent part of their summer on the run here, posing as newlyweds Lloyd and Lucy Johnson.[394] Be sure to check out Agnes and Whit Whitaker's barn, where "Lloyd and Lucy" hid out for a night upon their arrival.

Feeling hungry? Grab a bite at Ma and Pop Calhoun's Diner, where "Lucy" worked as a waitress and "Lloyd" was a short-order cook.[395] Plenty of souvenirs are available at Clem Briggs's General Store. You'll be walking the quaint streets where Luke and Laura befriended Sally and Hutch, unaware they were assassins sent by Frank Smith to take them out![396] If you're feeling particularly adventurous, 150 miles farther south you'll find Fair Oaks, New York, the home of the statue of the Left-Handed Boy, which provided the key to unlocking Frank Smith's "little black book." The winding roads can make it a lengthy drive, so you may want to spend the night at a motel on your way back. Just be sure to ask the manager for the "Wall of Jericho" Special!

PORT CHARLES MAYORAL MANSION

Once Luke and Laura unraveled the secrets of the little black book, they were able to defeat Frank and return home—where they faced a new kind of harassment from nosy reporters. Laura broke Luke's heart when she told them that, despite running off with him, she still considered herself Scotty Baldwin's wife.[397] Laura explained to Luke that she wanted her divorce from Scott to be final before they pursued a relationship.

By the time they saved the world from the Summer Blizzard of '81, Luke and Laura were heralded as heroes by the citizens of Port Charles. They announced their intention to get married, with Laura filing for a quickie divorce in Mexico. Luke and Laura were gifted with a lavish wedding at the mayoral mansion, to which the wedding party was driven in antique cars. The pristine grounds surrounding the ornate, stone mansion were the perfect location for their special day![398] Thankfully, Laura and I had buried the hatchet[399] by this point and I served as one of her bridesmaids, along with Claudia Johnston and Tiffany Hill,[400] with Laura's adoptive sister, Amy Vining, serving as maid of honor.

---

[393] Editor's note: Hit Route 31. It'll take you anywhere you need to be.

[394] Lucy's note: "Though I hadn't yet moved to Port Charles, I was the original Lucy."

[395] Says Robert S, "I sure hope Luke wore a hairnet to tame that beastly mane of his!"

[396] Editor's note: Amelia Joffe analyzes the assumed identity of Sally in her course "Gender Identity and Port Charles Politics of LGBT Appropriation."

[397] Says Scott, "By this point I'd left town with my tail between my legs. I was all over the place, can't say where I was at the time exactly. Texas, maybe?"

[398] Says current first lady Olivia Falconeri-Quartermaine, "Available now for bookings! Seriously, Ned and I don't even live there!"

[399] Adds Laura, "And not even in each other's backs."

[400] Editor's note: Star of such films as *You Only Schvitz Thrice*, *Death Comes to Duluth*, and *Christina Comes Home for Purim*.

As his groomsmen, Luke had Bryan Phillips, Joe Kelly, and Slick by his side . . . with Robert Scorpio serving as best man.

It was a beautiful ceremony! It felt like a thousand people were there![401] The festivities did not last long, however, as Scotty crashed the ceremony and caught Laura's bouquet. He revealed that he and Laura were still technically married! After some convincing, Scotty agreed to grant Laura a divorce. She and Luke became husband and wife. But a happy ending was not around the corner.

THE HAUNTED STAR[402]

I'd be remiss not to mention another guest at the wedding, albeit one who watched the ceremony from a distance—because she wasn't invited (and if she'd shown her face, someone might have ripped it off). Helena Cassadine, the widow of Mikkos,[403] left two peculiar gifts to the couple. The first was Mikkos's yacht, the *Titan*, which Luke and Laura rechristened the *Haunted Star*. The *Haunted Star* would change hands a number of times over the years, serving as everything from a cabaret to a casino. Recently, my niece Lulu has transformed it into Port Charles's hottest nightclub.[404] Their second present was something they desperately wanted to return, but Helena wasn't in the business of enclosing gift receipts—and I'm not sure they'd have been interested in an equal exchange.

Channeling generations of Cassadine family tradition, Helena cursed Luke and Laura, vowing that the couple would never enjoy their much-deserved lifetime of happiness. If you're a superstitious person, the curse worked. If you don't believe in that bunk, it was just dumb luck. A few short months later Laura was abducted. Luke, Robert, and the Webber family searched high and low for poor Laura. It wasn't long before she was presumed dead, a victim of the deranged David Gray.[405] But all was not as it appeared to be. A year later, Laura returned home, alive—but not exactly well. She'd escaped imprisonment on Cassadine Island by Helena's lustful son Stavros, who had fallen in love with her from afar and was determined to make her his—and would remain so for many years and through several deaths yet to come.

[401] Editor's note: Some claim it was more like thirty million.

[402] 100 Commodore Way, Pier 23, Berth 2

[403] Editor's note: Ye of the alleged "carbonic" snow.

[404] Happy hour from 5–7; $5 Malibu Sunsets, $4 draft beer; tell 'em Barbara Jean sent you for another 10 percent off!

[405] Says Luke S, "The cult of Malkuth—don't ask—thought Gray was the second coming of their God. Zuul, Zenu, whoever. He went out to loot the Port Charles Museum of antiquities he thought would prove their claim. Somewhere along the way he got my Laura confused with another Laura, one he thought might undo his scheme. He hypnotized my Laura and sent her out to sea."

DETOUR

CASSADINE ISLAND: I will deny ever saying this, but the Quartermaines would be considered "new money" compared to the Cassadines.[406] Mikkos and Helena were in control of a vast fortune, which included not one but two private islands. The island off the coast of South America was seized by the WSB after the Ice Princess debacle. The original island off the Greek mainland, however, remains in the family to this day. I would caution against visiting this island, as it is private property and known to have a sensitive and unforgiving security system. That being said, its warren of villas and beautiful beaches are the stuff of legend . . . and much Onassis jealousy!

Sadly, Laura didn't enjoy her time on this Mediterranean jewel. Stavros had given her an impossible choice: be his prisoner or be his wife. Given those options, it wasn't much of a choice. She conceived a child with Stavros, whom they named Nikolas. Privately, Laura shared her hopes and fears with Stavros's brother[407] Stefan.[408] With his encouragement, she managed to escape the island . . . but had no choice but to leave her infant son behind. It would be many years before she told Luke of poor Nikolas's existence.

> *Luke and Laura decided they could no longer run from their troubles*

CHARLES FALLS

After returning home to Port Charles and reuniting with her husband, Laura and Luke picked up stakes and set off to see the world. But it wasn't one extended vacation; they were doing their best to keep their heads down and out of sight from the rogues' gallery of enemies they'd amassed over the years. Along with their son, Lucky, they opened the Triple L Diner in British Columbia, Canada. Their happiness was short-lived again though when Frank Smith's minions tracked them down, setting off a car bomb outside the diner that might have killed them all.

Luke and Laura decided they could no longer run from their troubles. It was time to turn and face them head-on, and in the place they knew best: Port Charles. They sent Lucky ahead on his own, believing he'd be safer away from the targets on their backs.

---

[406] Says Tracy Q, "Better than 'no money,' Barbara Jean."

[407] Asks Lucy, "Are you going to tell them, Bobbie? Or shall I?"

[408] Responds Bobbie, "Do you want to write this tour, Lucy? I was briefly Stefan's wife. I was extremely vulnerable to Stefan's advances, reeling off finding my husband, Tony in bed with a woman who later turned out to be my daughter. I didn't heed my brother's warnings that the only good Cassadine is a Cassadine impaled through the heart, and I paid for it. While we're on the subject of bad romances, how's *your* love life these days, Lucy?"

Luke stole a plane in hopes of getting to Port Charles before Frank Smith's men caught up to them again.

My brother is many things. An experienced pilot is not one of them. They made it to Port Charles—but only after the plane ran out of gas and they had to parachute into the wild Port Charles River . . . which fed right into the nearby Charles Falls! If not for the timely arrival of a rescue chopper and its trusty rope ladder plucking Luke and Laura from the river, they'd surely be fish food today. Instead they were dumped by a pool at a country club, interrupting a wedding reception. Near-death experiences aside, Charles Falls is one of the truly great natural wonders of PC.[409]

CHARLES STREET

Our last stop on the tour brings us to the historic Charles Street District. Early in our fair city's history, the dockworkers who helped turn Port Charles into a bustling metropolis called Charles Street their home. The largely Victorian homes were a haven for working-class people of diverse backgrounds at a time when plenty of areas of the country were far less welcoming. While drying themselves off from their Charles Falls excursion, Luke and Laura discovered a beautiful abandoned house on Charles Street. Laura immediately fell in love with the place, and soon made it her home. Here Luke and Laura spent the next few years hatching new businesses[410] and raising Lucky, along with a daughter soon to come, Lulu.

Together and with their new friend, the late Mary Mae Ward, they became community activists, fighting ELQ efforts to place a toxic waste incinerator in their sometimes disadvantaged neighborhood. But the good times yet again did not last long for Luke and Laura. They were under constant assault from one enemy[411] or another,[412] and the strain of Stefan's arrival with Laura's never-mentioned son, Nikolas (to say nothing of Luke's distaste for a life of quiet domesticity[413]), was too much for even this legendary couple to endure. Luke and Laura parted ways, but their legacy lives on around every corner in town!

> *Luke and Laura parted ways, but their legacy lives on . . .*

---

[409] Lucy's pro tip: "You'll find a spectacular view from a hidden footbridge nearby. But if you a see a brooding man in a black T-shirt there, give him his space!"

[410] Editor's note: Luke opened a successful blues club, which played host to a number of fabled acts. The club no longer exists, having burned to the ground years ago. Today in its place stands the Ava Jerome Gallery.

[411] Editor's note: Frank Smith and his son Damian.

[412] Editor's note: Joe Scully.

[413] Editor's note: And the couple coming to terms with what happened at the Campus Disco years before . . .

"DON'T KNOW MUCH ABOUT HISTORY" HEROES FROM PORT CHARLES'S PAST

For those history buffs out there, you also might want to visit some spots that relate to the following folks who have contributed not just to Port Charles over the years, but literally the world at large too.[414]

[414] Editor's note: Special thanks to the Port Charles Historical Society (located at 152 Main Street) for access to primary source documents that helped make these characters from the past come alive.

ALICE IMOGEN WEBBER

Although she worked alongside Elizabeth Cady Stanton and Susan B. Anthony, a name lost to history was Port Charles's own Alice Imogen Webber. Alice was most famous for attempting to enroll in medical school in an attempt to be the first female surgeon. (She never achieved this goal when her medical school was burned to the ground during the Draft Riots of 1863.)

She's also famous for her 1855 marriage ceremony that renounced the legal rights that men usually gained over their wives upon such unions, and for keeping her own last name after marriage. After her husband's death in 1877, Alice moved back to Port Charles from New York City and is buried in the Port Charles graveyard. Young surgeons can now often be seen leaving a clementine (her favorite fruit) on her grave after finishing their residencies.

EDGAR ALAN QUARTERMAINE

Did you know that the "Father of Civil War Battlefield Medicine" was a Quartermaine? At least that's what Edgar Quartermaine dubbed himself in his memoir, *A Quarter Till Midnight*. Born in Port Charles, Edgar wrote how, after the Battle of Gettysburg, he developed what became known as the spiral tourniquet used during battlefield amputations to control bleeding. [Editor's note: This has never been confirmed; some facts are simply lost to history.] After the war, Edgar claims his ne'er-do-well brother, Elijah, attempted to patent it and sell it to hospitals in the Western territories. Perhaps the first recorded instance of Quartermaine family squabbling?

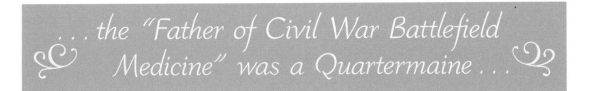

. . . the "Father of Civil War Battlefield Medicine" was a Quartermaine . . .

CAPTAIN JEREMIAH

Much is known of the acts of treason committed by Benedict Arnold, but did you know that Port Charles has its own connection to Colonial treachery? In 1780, Captain Jerome was feeling very bitter toward the Continental Congress. His discontent was because no members of the Congress had attended his nuptials to Olive Devane, on account that she was the British daughter of the Duke of Salisbury and rumored spy. Appointed as the commander of the fort at Port Charles, New York, Jerome offered to leave it unguarded for Olive's British relatives to take over for a large sum of money.

Jerome's plan was discovered, by a quick-thinking young Italian merchant named Giuseppe Falconeri, who overheard the plot in a pub. Jerome quickly swore allegiance to the British and commanded British forces in several small-scale battles, all of which, he lost. By 1783, America was free and although he missed his new hometown of Port Charles, he and Olive could never go back. He died in 1808, penniless. A landscape belonging to Olive and Jeremiah, that now hangs in the British Museum, is said to be their favorite view: that of Port Charles at dawn.

LYLE THOMAS HARDY

Renegade pilot Lyle Thomas Hardy is often thought of as America's greatest "balloon buster," a nickname assigned to the brash aviators who attacked German observation balloons used to sight artillery during World War I. Lyle joined the 24th Aero Squadron in France in August 1918, and wasted little time exasperating other pilots with his cocky attitude and rash flying style. He even had the phrase, "Hard-ier then You All" painted on the side of his plane. The Port Charles-born aviator, however, proved an expert at downing the reconnaissance balloons and made a name for himself worldwide. He became the seventh pilot to receive the Medal of Honor (a fact that is noted on his grave . . . to some's chagrin, because who wants to be the seventh at anything?)

"MOONSHINE MAUDE" SPENCER

Any teenager at PC High will tell you about the age-old graduation tradition of going out to the Catacombs on the last day of school, in search of the secret liquor that's said to be buried there. The booze in question was reportedly left by the legendary "Moonshine Maude" Spencer. Spencer initially created a distillery in the claw-footed bathtub in her cabin as a means of attempting to cure a nasty cough (or so she said).

Maude's product became so popular, however, that she couldn't keep up with demand. She began to import whiskey from Canada via tugboats making their way down the Charles River (some still say they see her ghost on the banks of the water, waiting for shipments). After being arrested by Sheriff Zebadiah McBain, Maude is said to have hid twelve crates of crème de menthe in the Catacombs exclaiming, "You can take me, but you'll never find my hooch." She was sentenced to church every Sunday for four years at her bootlegging trial in 1928. In the last pew of the church you can see the etchings where she marked each day.

NATALIE "NAT" REEVES

Though historians have long argued about the validity of her dissents claim, we here in town believe that the very first Pony Express rider, Natalie "Nat" Reeves, was born in Port Charles in 1827. Never comfortable in a corset and pantaloons, fourteen-year-old Natalie cut off her hair, put on a pair of britches, and told her brothers, "Call me Nat." Her family were struggling potato farmers in a region that did not support the growth of tubers, so Nat decided a fortune was to be made in the wave of the future: equestrian mail delivery. Attempting to compete with the Erie Canal, Nat wrote her mother, Augusta, "Don't worry Mama, I can get mail to western New York faster than any mule." Nat proved to be successful for a time, until she and her horse were stopped in their tracks, literally, by a New York City-bound train. Still young, Nat planted the seeds of the Reeves fortune, and perhaps Nina Reeves's obsession with horses.

SWEETIE WARD

Little is known of silent movie star Sweetie Ward's childhood, as her age was constantly changed to keep up with the demand of the tastes of the day. Her big break was playing Pocahontas in the short *New World, for Who?* Sweetie continued making historically themed epics with the Quarter-Que Film Corp in New York.

When talking pictures became the rage, however, Sweetie was forced to retire due to a childhood stutter that she was never able to overcome. Legend has it that she told the ticket clerk at Grand Central Station to give her a one-way ticket to a place with trees, water, and music—and he sent her to Port Charles. Sweetie lived the last few years of her life on the waterfront, and when autograph seekers would bring old *Photoplay* magazines, she would refuse to sign them stating, "That's not me, it's just a girl I used to know with similar features." When film students at PCU discovered old reels of her work, they started the annual Sweetie Shorts in Winter Festival, which showcases her work.[415]

SVEN CUMMINGS

Best known for adding cocoa beans with coffee beans, and creating the world first café mocha, Sven Cummings actually has roots in Port Charles. Tired of the limited spice palate in his native Norway, Sven and his band of merry wanderers, known as the "Flavor Pirates," stumbled upon Port Charles in 1615. Upon landing, Sven met Gaspard Charles; his diaries reflect that he was not impressed: "This man is as bland as butter in England."

Sven, however, was duly enchanted by a member of Charles's party, a lovely lass named Clara Jones. Clara had the only refined palate in her camp, and enchanted Sven with her ability to make a flavorful tea out of stalk-weeds. Sven went so far as to attempt to convince Clara to go seek their fortune west, but Clara was already promised to another (Port Charles's first case of star-crossed lovers waiting for history to correct their mistake with future generations?). After his stint in Port Charles, Cummings's diaries indicate he made his way to Mexico, where he fell in love with an Aztec princess.

LILLIAN MORGAN

Known as "New York's Edison," Lillian had a hand in patenting over 175 inventions in her nineteenth-century laboratory (which was located right behind the emergency room of General Hospital). Some of her most notable creations include inflatable water floaties, an early can opener that used literal horsepower to pry open anything, and (my favorite) an umbrella that had a snap-on cloth clover that allowed for it to be color-coordinated.

On what would have been her hundredth birthday, her granddaughter, Lila Morgan Quartermaine, christened the children's playroom at General Hospital "The Morgan Explorium."

---

[415] The discovery of these shorts led to the founding of the Port Charles International Film Festival.

WHAT TO SEE, WHAT TO DO

Other hometown cheerleaders may be content to give you the skinny on the best places to hike or to tuck into overpriced artisanal pizza, but I'm not your average hometown cheerleader. My readers deserve better. Port Charles deserves better! While you'll absolutely find that information here,[416] I want you all to get the full portrait on why Port Charles is more than a place you should visit, and a place you should make your home.

---

[416] For the best pizza in town, order the Lucy in the Pie with Diamonds special at Pozzulo's. Pozzulo's is owned and operated by the Corinthos Group. It is located on the west side of Port Charles, at 820 South Clinton Avenue. Pozzulo's does not deliver; reservations recommended, as hours can be erratic. Call 716-555-PIES.

SPOON ISLAND

Shakespeare once wrote, "Marry, he must have a long spoon that must eat with the devil."[417] You can read a lot into that quote, and it perfectly describes our next exotic locale, Spoon Island. Spoon Island was bought from the city of Port Charles in 1882 by the fabulously rich Washington Wyndham, founder of Wyndham's Department Store. It was on the island that he then built his dream home, the estate of Wyndemere.[418] The historical record tells us that many residents and folklorists warned Wash not to buy the island, as legend long had it that it was an unlucky place.[419]

Despite the warnings,[420] Wyndham went ahead and built his dream home. Wyndemere's conveniences were practically unheard of at the time of its construction. These novel structural elements included steam and forced-air heating, indoor plumbing, push-button gas lights, and a shower in Mr. Wyndham's suite (that also featured self-heating water). The constant construction and lack of a master building plan resulted, however, in a large and disjointed house, which soon became the talk of Port Charles. Newspaper accounts of the time noted that serving staff needed a map to navigate their way through each room of the manor.[421] As Wyndham aged into his dotage, he became convinced that the house was haunted by the former inhabitants of the island, who were trying to drive him away and retake their ancestral home. Wyndham decided that the house should have only one working bathroom for himself, and that all the other restrooms were to be made "decoys" to confuse the spirits.

He also attempted to hide from "angry ghosts" by sleeping in a different bedroom each night. It seemed he couldn't outlast what haunted him for long, as Washington Wyndham was found dead on the eve of his sixty-sixth birthday. His butler, Jackson Ward, found him sprawled in the entranceway clutching two candlesticks and the deed to the house. Trying to appease a visitor from the hereafter, perhaps?

After Wyndham's death the house fell into disrepair and the island and estate went largely uninhabited, though for a time it was owned and lived in by Iona Huntington.[422]

Ned Ashton[423] failed to learn from the mistakes of Charles or Wyndham and purchased the island and Wyndemere as a present for his fiancée, Dawn Winthrop. But their happiness was short-lived. Their engagement was called off and their relationship soon imploded when Dawn realized Ned had previously[424] had an affair

---

[417] Lucy's note: YES I know SHAKESPEARE. I was a librarian once upon a time.

[418] Editor's note: No address needed beyond "Wyndemere, Spoon Island." A helpful hint: best to leave Wyndemere's inhabitants off your holiday greeting card list. USPS refuses to set foot on the island.

[419] Editor's note: Like Gaspard Charles before him, Wyndham failed to heed warnings that all those who attempted to settle the island were summarily jinxed.

[420] Editor's note: Or perhaps because of them?

[421] Excerpted from the recovered diary of Mariah Gunderson, an original servant at Wyndemere, "The house has doors that open into walls, a staircase that leads nowhere and everything is in groups of thirteen. Saints preserve me!"

[422] Editor's note: Iona Huntington was a talented counterfeiter and also the aunt of famed pianist and former flame of Robert Scorpio, Katherine Delafield. Iona briefly returned to Wyndemere to collect a counterfeiting machine she'd secreted away there.

[423] Editor's note: Ashton, who has since taken his mother's maiden name, was elected mayor in 2018.

[424] Lucy's note: While working as a country club tennis pro.

with her mother, Monica.[425] Dawn was later murdered and Ned endured two horrendous marriages, so you'd think that people might then have gotten the idea—stay off Spoon Island!

But Cesar Faison just had to have it. As referenced elsewhere, Faison was horny for Lumina crystals and believed he might find some on the island. Maybe if he'd just rented a cottage on the mainland he'd have turned out okay. But it wasn't too long after his stay on Wyndemere that he was presumed dead in a missile strike.

A few years later still more settlers showed up on Spoon Island—specifically Stefan and Prince Nikolas Cassadine.[426] For a time it seemed that Spoon Island's luck might be changing—and then Stefan went and accidentally shot Katherine Bell.[427] Incredibly, Stefan and Katherine got over this and threw a traditional Bacchanalia Ball[428] to announce their engagement.

But the bad juju soon reasserted itself when Katherine fell from a parapet to her death at her very own party. Ironically, Stefan himself later died of a fall there, too. After Stefan's demise, his nephew Nikolas realized his family was deeply[429] in debt. Nikolas's aunt Alexis Davis convinced him that selling Wyndemere was the only thing to be done. But Nikolas's true love, Emily Quartermaine, rode to the rescue, finally answering this age-old question: What do you get the prince who has everything? Emily bought back the house and regifted it to Nikolas for Christmas.[430] To try to erase the memories of all this death and destruction, Nikolas offered to host Lucky and Elizabeth's long overdue wedding.

But as Washington Wyndham came to learn, the spirit of the island did not believe that happiness had a right to exist on stolen land. Right after the ceremony the groom and several of the wedding party were injured in a train crash, putting a damper on the festivities. Ignoring all these premonitions of doom, Nikolas threw caution to the wind and threw a ball to celebrate his engagement to Emily Quartermaine. But that same wind blew

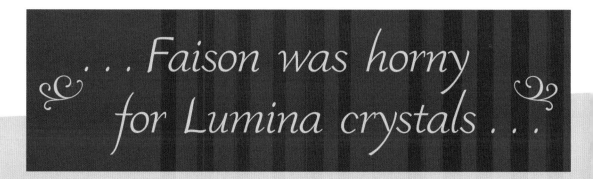

. . . Faison was horny for Lumina crystals . . .

[425] Lucy's note: Although it's my understanding the affair was over and done with before Ned got together with Dawn, so I don't see what her problem was. Aside from the general shiver-inducing knowledge that your fiancé slept with your mother. Okay, I guess that's problem enough.

[426] Editor's note: It is understood from political machinations over the years that the Cassadine title of Prince passes from eldest son to eldest son. If a Cassadine Prince dies without a male heir, the title dies with him and the fortune he controlled is scattered amongst the surviving family members.

[427] Lucy's note: The editor insisted I word it like that, but I only agreed to on the condition I got this footnote. As far as I'm concerned, Katherine's shooting was proof that Spoon Island was finally doing the people of Port Charles some good!

[428] Editor's note: The Bacchanalia Ball, is based in Russian traditions and is a masquerade ball thrown in honor of a Cassadine engagement.

[429] Says Luke S, "Didn't Stefan know how much overhead comes with the operation of secret labs, carbonic snow, and Lazarus pits?"

[430] Lucy's note: "If only she'd read her Port Charles history!"

in and stranded everyone on the island—with creepy Anthony Zacchara. Daddy Z attacked several guests and killed a groundskeeper, all while staying hidden in the shadows.[431] If Zacchara's dastardly deeds weren't cause for enough misery, there was still one murder to go: Nikolas's bride-to-be, Emily, was strangled in the house by the Text Message Killer, Diego Alcazar.

Finally realizing that Wyndemere might not be the best place to raise his son,[432] Nikolas moved off the island. During the next few years, the island's spirits attracted an array of no-goodniks like "Mother of the Year" Helena Cassadine, who there murdered her own daughter, Irina, and Caleb Morley,[433] who suffered under the delusion that he was a vampire.[434] Yes.[435] A vampire.[436] But Caleb[437] was defeated[438] when I single-handedly[439] rescued Sam Morgan and her little boy.

Proving you can't keep a prince away from his haunted castle, Nikolas and his son, Spencer, moved back to Wyndemere in 2013. The lessons of the past had yet to be learned. Nikolas agreed to host his mother Laura's wedding to Scott Baldwin. Later international bad guy Jerry Jax employed blackmail to force Nikolas to play landlord to Robin Scorpio-Drake, Britt Westbourne, Cesar Faison, and Liesl Obrecht all at the same time.[440]

Despite all odds, and a fire that temporarily scarred little Spencer's face,[441] the house and island entered into a time of seeming peace. Nikolas's mother, Laura, moved in. Nikolas married Hayden Barnes. Was the curse lifted? Were the spirits appeased? Ha! Nothing appeases a spirit! They're dead and stuck in the land of the living, doomed never to ascend to the next plane! They're pissed for all eternity! Proving that evil is genetic, the brooding Valentin Cassadine reared his closely coiffed head and extorted Nikolas into signing over the entire Cassadine estate. Not content with swindling all of his nephew's earthly possessions, Valentin shot Nikolas on Cassadine Island. The tragic prince stumbled off his balcony and fell to his death.[442] Currently, Valentin and his daughter Charlotte control the vast bulk of the Cassadine empire, as well as Spoon Island.

Want to know more? The Museum of Mayhem offers guided boat cruises around the island every summer Saturday and Sunday at 11:00 a.m. Tours depart from Pier 23 and are just $49.95, with a boxed lunch from Kelly's included.

---

[431] Lucy's note: Not hard to do in a place teeming with secret passages and easy access to catacombs.

[432] Editor's note: Nikolas's son, Spencer, was born as the result of an affair Nikolas had with Sonny Corinthos's half sister, Courtney Matthews.

[433] Lucy's note: Or was it rock star Stephen Clay?

[434] Asks Bobbie S, "Are you going to tell them, Lucy? Or shall I?"

[435] Lucy's note: Yes, fine, okay Bobbie. There was once a very short, teeny-weeny sliver of time when I too thought Caleb was a vampire.

[436] Presses Bobbie S, "And . . . ?"

[437] Lucy's note: I may have also once thought that a few other people were vampires, too—but I don't think those things anymore!"

[438] Comments Bobbie S, "The happy pills help with that, don't they?"

[439] Editor's note: While Ms. Coe was an integral part of the rescue mission, the now-deceased teen Rafe Kovich—son of Alison Barrington (and Llanview police transplant John McBain)—might have played an important role as well.

[440] Editor's note: Word is Disney has optioned this tale as a structure for an *Odd Couple* reboot starring Tiffany Hill as Obrecht.

[441] Opines Spencer, "Although I was upset that my imbecilic cousin Cameron Webber disfigured me, I have decided my scar is the mark of a romantic hero. When the time comes to return to Port Charles, I'll have Emma Scorpio-Drake eating out of the palm of my hand—and Cameron will be polishing my riding boots."

[442] Editor's Note: Ava Jerome witnessed Nikolas's fall, but his body never turned up, so for all we know he'll be back in town by next Founder's Day.

AMANDA BARRINGTON CENTER FOR THE ARTS

Since its opening in 1922, the Barrington[443] Center for the Arts[444] has been Port Charles's preeminent performance space. The magnificent theater, which originally contained 2,352 seats, was built by famed local architect Walter Quartermaine as a center for music, dance, and silent film (with live organ accompaniment). An architectural gem, its opulent Egyptian-inspired décor reflects the taste and elegance of New York's gilded age. During the golden age of the Broadway musical, the Barrington became the first touring stop after Broadway for such classic shows as *Gadzooks!*, *Brooklyn Is Not a Four-Letter Word*, *A Parisian in Port Charles*, and a holiday tradition to this day, *Christina Comes Home for Christmas*.

Today the center still hosts touring productions and visiting artists like Katherine Delafield[445] and is used throughout the year by a variety of community organizations for lectures and other special events (such as the *Crimson Magazine*–sponsored Fashion Show showcasing local designers). The Barrington Center is also the home of both the Port Charles Philharmonic and the Port Charles Ballet. A smaller theater, known as the Alison Barrington[446] Black Box, officially

---

[443] Named for the Grover Barrington, of Barrington Baby Formula fame. Later donations were made by Barrington heiress Amanda and F.O.Q. (friend of Quartermaine).

[444] Located at 26 Gibbs Street. Box office hours 10–6 Monday–Friday, 11–3 weekends. Call 716-555-TIXX to order over the phone.

[445] Says Robert S, "Katherine is a world-class pianist and pain in my rear. She's also one of the classiest dames I've ever had the honor to protect from assassination . . . or wind up hanging from the side of a Marriott hotel sign ten stories up.

[446] Editor's note: Named for Amanda's granddaughter. Alison was murdered in 2013 by a man suffering from delusions that he was a vampire. The following year Alison's surviving son, teenager Rafe Kovich Jr, died of injuries sustained in a car crash—but not before his heart was transplanted to Alice Gunderson, trusty Quartermaine maid. Thus, Alison and Rafe were in a way F.O.Q.'s, just like their predecessor.

opened in 2009. The Black Box features a two-hundred-seat theater, which is used by Port Charles University[447] for student productions and is home to the Port Charles Players (PCP) community theater group. Recent PCP productions have included *The Odd Couple,* starring GH head nurse Epiphany Johnson and GH chief of staff Monica Quartermaine, and a feminist take on *Twelve Angry Men,* re-titled *Twelve Angry Women* (starring Alexis Davis[448] and Diane Miller, among other luminaries of Port Charles's amateur actors). Particularly well received was a recent production of *The Sound of Music,* starring Dr. Liesl Obrecht[449] as Maria and Mac Scorpio as Captain Von Trapp.

PORT CHARLES AMPHITHEATER

Built in 1982 during the first phase of a waterfront revitalization project, this ten-thousand-seat open-air venue—the first of its kind in the Port Charles area—hosts a mixture of concerts, family programming, and comedy shows. Right on the river, it incorporated the famed turn-of-the-century Brewer Brewing Company building into its design. The amphitheater has hosted such diverse acts as Eli Love, Eddie Maine and the Idle Rich, Frisco Jones, and was one of the first venues to host worldwide phenomenon Miguel Morez.

FLOYD FIELD

Built in 2007 with funds raised by, you guessed it, none other than our infamous former mayor, Garrett Prescott "Pres" Floyd, Floyd Field is home to the two-time Triple-A national champion Port Charles Woodchucks baseball team. Despite its dubious origins, Floyd Field is much better known for its many unique ballpark features, including the Floyd Fun Zone, which is a perfect pit stop for visiting families (with its "Sport Court" basketball court, rock climbing wall, bungee trampoline, simulated pitching area, and hospital-themed playground). In left field, they have rocking chairs right under the Home Run Porch (come early to snag one, they've proven to be quite popular with our geriatric set). In light of revelations of Floyd's corruption and adultery,[450] the city is said to be mulling offers for name-change bids, so stay tuned for a potential rechristening of this hallowed Triple-A stadium.

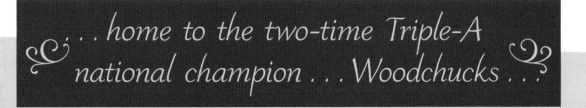

. . . home to the two-time Triple-A national champion . . . Woodchucks . . .

---

[447] Admissions and offices of the president and dean of students are located at 631 University Drive.

[448] Says Julian J, "More like *Eleven Angry Women and One Fascinating Goddess.*"

[449] Says Anna D, "Perhaps the closest Liesl has ever been to God."

[450] Editor's note: With none other than legal eagle and winner of the Chuckie Award for her portrayal of Juror #9 in the PCP production of *Twelve Angry Women,* Alexis Davis.

PORT CHARLES BOTANICAL SOCIETY

The PCBS (don't let the initials fool you, it smells lovely) states on its brochure that "The mission of the Port Charles Botanical Society[451] is to foster education of both area and exotic flora and fauna, and to preserve and maintain the historic Port Charles University campus built around the original greenhouse." The PCBS is the place to go to if you're looking for an escape from the hospital, your family, and/or both. It is also the spot where I frequented in search of fragrance notes for my Deception Cosmetics[452] creations.

Watch out for rotating specialty exhibits such as "Flowers of the Caribbean" (sponsored by Corinthos Coffee) and the "Bursts of Red" rose show (sponsored by *Crimson Magazine*). The PCBS is also the home of the world-renowned Quartermaine Shakespearean garden, which was the location of one of my favorite weddings not my own: that of Robert Scorpio to Anna Devane.[453]

PORT CHARLES MUSEUM OF NATURAL HISTORY AND PLANETARIUM

The permanent and traveling exhibits at the Port Charles Museum of Natural History[454] claim to "illustrate and interpret science and the natural world to visitors. Dioramas allow visitors to experience the past and explore how life was lived on Marie Charles's original settlement. (Hint: not fun. Turns out manual labor like husking corn is hell on a manicure.) Explore the Lila Quartermaine Gallery of Gems & Jewels, where much of a famous (or infamous) cache of Aztec treasure[455] is on permanent display. You can also check out the re-created Aztec Temple, which has become a popular spot of local teens to take pre-prom pictures. The attached Planetarium features an award-winning show about the exploration of space and galaxies far and near, with a spotlight on Proxima Centauri and the planet Lumina. It's narrated by none other than Dr. Robin Scorpio-Drake.[456]

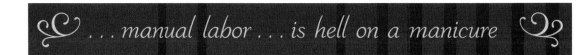

. . . manual labor . . . is hell on a manicure

[451] The PCBS is located at 500 University Drive.

[452] Lucy's note: R.I.P.

[453] Lucy's note: I never actually received an invitation, but I'm sure that was just an oversight. It was a lovely, amazing, gorgeous, English garden of a wedding—except for the part when my friend Dominque heard the toll of some bells, causing her to have a psychotic flashback and pull a gun. Or the part when international terrorist Cesar Faison showed up to try to whisk Anna away. The important thing is, when Anna tossed her bouquet, I was the one to catch it! So stick it where the sun doesn't shine, Tracy Q!

[454] The Port Charles Museum of Natural History and Planetarium is located at 1100 Ontario Avenue.

[455] Lucy's note: Donated by Mariah Ramirez, grandmother to longtime Port Charles resident, my friend, bartender/private investigator/writer/interior designer Felicia Scorpio. How blond-haired, blue-eyed Felicia turned out to be descended from Aztec royalty is beyond me.

[456] Editor's note: Strangely knowledgeable for a medical doctor on matters of the cosmos.

PORT CHARLES MUSEUM OF FINE ART—"THE CHUCK"

Perhaps the most venerable Port Charles institution is the Museum of Fine Art—or, "the Chuck."[457] This landmark building, designed to resemble a swan, is a must-see for any visitor with a more refined palate. Ava Jerome[458] currently chairs the board, and her tenure has been controversial, as she has favored presenting artists of a more, er, challenging breed.[459] The museum has many fine pieces, but is best known for its impressionist collection, which includes works by lesser-known artistic siblings, Claudia Monet and Roberto Renoir. Be sure to take in *Summer in Provence*, a painting so lovely and coveted it is said to have inspired a blood feud between two notoriously testy collectors, Bill Eckert and Richard Halifax.

Among Ms. Jerome's more recent endeavors at the Chuck was a joint exhibit with the Museum of Mayhem entitled "Sandwich Fever: The Watercolor Works of Heather Webber." This particular exhibit has been protested daily by PCMAN, Port Charles Mothers Against the Normalization of Violence.[460] For those with kiddies, Elizabeth Webber runs a family Friday art clinic on the first Saturday of every month.

MUSEUM OF MAYHEM

If crime scenes are more your thing than watercolors, head over to the Museum of Mayhem. Located five blocks from General Hospital at 6500 Central Avenue, the museum's brochure states that they seek to "provide an interactive journey through the darker side of Port Charles."[461] The most popular exhibits require separate admission, so get there early to try to see if you can beat Heather Webber's time for escaping a Shadybrook straitjacket —less than a minute! In my favorite attraction, "Satan's Leash," one attempts to outwit evil, crazy, crazy-evil Grant Putnam's cuddly but famished guard Rottweiler named, you guessed it, Satan. I'm proud to say I hold both records[462]—at the museum, and in real life (regarding the straitjacket; you'll have to ask Anna Devane about the dog).[463] Be sure to check out the museum's latest exhibition, "The Many Faces of Cesar Faison," featuring not only the deceased former director of the DVX's[464] collection of masks (the "Duke Lavery"—or what's left of it[465]—gives me nightmares) but also such notable mementos as his formula for carbon disulfide, the most "deadly nerve

---

[457] The Chuck is located just down the street from the Museum of Natural History at 1200 Ontario Avenue.

[458] Says Carly C, "When she's not trying to beat the charges."

[459] Including none other than a "rehabilitated" serial killer, Franco.

[460] Says current PCPD police commissioner Jordan Ashford, "They have their work cut out for them."

[461] Says Scott B, "For Sonny Corinthos that's any given Tuesday."

[462] Editor's note: This has not been substantiated.

[463] Says Anna D, "That guard dog was the closest I'll ever come to being a pet owner."

[464] Editor's note: The international criminal spy gang. To this day the meaning of the acronym DVX is a closely held government secret.

[465] Faison spent one stint in Port Charles impersonating Anna Devane's presumed-dead husband, Duke Lavery. His plot to bamboozle Anna into marriage was uncovered by Robert Scorpio when he threw a pot of fondue oil on his face, thus melting the latex Duke mask and revealing the monster beneath.

gas known to mankind"; Jenny Eckert's "bomb" wedding bouquet; and first editions of his literary endeavors, *The Crystalline Conspiracy* and *The Alpine Express*.[466]

Take a break from all the mayhem and enjoy a treat in the attached Ice Princess Ice Cream Palace, which features such treats as Mikkos's Marshmallow Mudslide and a Stellar Stavros Sundae. When you're ready to get back to exploring all the calamity Port Charles has been subjected to over the years, check out more recent acquisitions (or replicas) of the following: Ryan Chamberlain's knife; the cell phone used by Diego Alcazar (aka the Text Message Killer); and original "artwork" by pre-tumor-removal Franco.[467] The Mob

Laser Shoot-Out room was a popular spot for children's birthday parties, until last year when PCMAN staged a die-in, prompting the museum to restrict entrance to all but those over the age of eighteen. Construction of a new wing housing an IMAX theater is almost complete. Scuttlebutt is that the theater's inaugural screening will be an interactive adventure called *Bombs Away: Port Charles's Greatest Explosions*. Visit the museum while you still can: its owners are currently under threat of legal action from Sonny Corinthos— "coffee importer"—for a proposed virtual reality day-in-the-life attraction based on his history as a simple entrepreneur just trying to make an honest buck.

> *Take a break from all the mayhem and enjoy a treat in the attached Ice Princess Ice Cream Palace . . .*

---

[466] Editor's note: Written under the nom de plume "P. K. Sinclair," these books follow the exploits of a central heroine named Davnee—which happens to be an anagram for "Devane."

[467] Says Jason M, "It's amazing no one has burned that place down yet."

PORT CHARLES ZOO

The Port Charles Zoo[468] recently celebrated its fiftieth anniversary with the grand opening of the "Wolf Woods," an enclosure that exhibits the lives of a small pack of tundra wolves. The enclosure—sponsored by the Corinthos Coffee Company[469]—features glass panels that allow visitors to feel like a member of the pack. An array of viewing stations also let you see the wolves[470] from many vantage points. Port Charles Zoo has re-created Florida's wooded wetlands for your encounter with an animal that remains unchanged after millions of years—and I'm not talking about Monica Quartermaine. What prehistoric reptile can lie camouflaged underneath the water's surface for as long as two hours but still have enough strength to catch and devour a deer? If your answer is Luke Spencer, you're not wrong, but I'm referring to Alligator Alley,[471] located right next to the food court.

CANNERY THEATER

A new attraction getting a ton of buzz is the Cannery Theater, right in the center of the redeveloped waterfront. An old cannery[472] has been repurposed as an interactive dinner theater installation space. The "Cans," as the troupe's actors call themselves, are currently presenting the *Cartel Experience*.[473] *Cartel* is a fully immersive show that invites the audience to experience in a frightfully firsthand way the shocking history of the carbon disulfide disaster that almost befell our fair city.[474]

[468] The Port Charles Zoo is located at just inside the city limits at 3000 Canterbury Avenue.

[469] Comments PCPD police commissioner Jordan Ashford, "And without a hint of irony, either."

[470] Says Bobbie S, "Lucy feels right at home at the wolf exhibit. She learned all her best grooming secrets from the pack."

[471] Lucy's note: A gift from the gone and best-forgotten Damian "Slime" Smith, preppy son of gangster and perpetual adversary of Luke and Laura Spencer, Frank Smith. Damian thought he could bed any woman he set his mind to, so I set my mind to bedding happily married Bobbie Jones. Well, Bobbie's last name is Spencer now, so you can imagine how that bet turned out. . . .

[472] Once owned by Barrett Industries, the cannery's true purpose was the manufacturing of the deadly carbon disulfide gas.

[473] Editor's note: Our coverage of Port Charles's annual Founder's Day celebration touches on the criminal cartel plot, and the heroism everyday Port Charlesers undertook to stop it.

[474] Editor's note: This is not recommended for children and easily triggered audiences, as strobe and gas effects are employed. Audience members are required to sign a waiver absolving the theater from responsibility for any injuries or deaths that occur as a result of the performance.

PORT CHARLES HALLOWEEN PET PARADE

One annual event that really shines my coat is the Port Charles Halloween Pet Parade, which takes place in the pediatrics ward on the fourth floor at General Hospital.[475] A menagerie of animals and their people from all over the wild kingdom don their best costumes and invade the hospital in an effort to bring smiles to young patients' faces. Come visit and I'm sure you'll agree with me that the old saying is true: pets match their people, whether they mean to or not! I'm looking at you Dr. Monica Quartermaine and Annabelle! Locals get pretty competitive for a chance to win the grand prize: their names and photos added to GH's "Hall of Fauna Fame." Highlights have included Lucky Spencer's mutt, Foster, done up as Al Capone; my duck, Sigmund, as a "Quack" doctor; Dr. Hamilton Finn's bearded dragon, Roxy, as a circus' bearded lady; and my personal fave, the first and only wallaby ever to be crowned champion, Ralph P. Scorpio, whom Holly Sutton entered dressed in a trench coat similar to the one favored by her true love, Robert Scorpio. And you thought the wildest Halloween parade was in Greenwich Village!

[475] 6065 Central Avenue

PORT CHARLES MAKER FAIRE

Part science fair, part county fair, all parking lot, the annual Port Charles Maker Faire is not to be missed. The Faire is held on the last weekend in March in the parking lot right behind General Hospital. It's an all-ages gathering of hobbyists and crafters, tinkerers and authors, artists and artisans, all of them "makers" of one thing or another, who gather to show off their wares and share how they do it. Recent participants have included Ava Jerome, whose "blow your own" martini glass station was a huge hit last year, and Olivia Falconeri-Quartermaine, whose stirring tomato sauce station features recipes from her self-published cookbook, *Falconeris Know Fettuccine*. This year's roster includes such diverse talent as everyone's favorite neurologist,[476] Dr. Griffin Munro. "Father" Munro[477] will operate a booth where he'll teach you how to make your own Advent calendars, customized for any holiday you might fancy. Rumors are swirling that the one and only Tiffany Hill[478] is set to grace the Faire with her presence, to lead a workshop on how to turn your home movies into modern masterpieces.

PORT CHARLES INTERNATIONAL FILM FESTIVAL

Watch out, Sundance! Sacrebleu, Cannes! Here comes Port Charles! The PCIFF is a juried film festival sponsored by Aurora Media and the Port Charles Chamber of Commerce. Held annually in the Amanda Barrington Center for the Arts, the PCIFF searches out only the most daring independent cinema. According to current organizers Nina Reeves[479] and Maxie Jones-West,[480] "The PCIFF proves to the world that this town has more to offer than gurneys and guns. We prove that auteurs can thrive anywhere, even in western New York!"

The festival began in 2008 when a group of Port Charles University film students lucked out on a box of old film reels in a little-visited stack in the school library. Just like all of my exes, they had an eye for treasure. Upon painstaking restoration, archivists discovered the reels contained the comedic shorts of forgotten silent film star Sweetie Ward.[481]

---

[476] Son of the deceased, tango-dancing, kilt-sporting, brogued Scottish mobster, debonair Duke Lavery.

[477] Lucy's note: In addition to being a brain doctor, Griffin is a priest—or, he was one. He recently gave up his collar when he could no longer deny his love—or is it lust?—for she-devil Ava Jerome.

[478] Star of such B movies as *The Shivering*, *It's Still Alive!*, and *My Coffin or Yours?*

[479] Editor of *Crimson Magazine*.

[480] Creative director of *Crimson Magazine*; also, sister-in-law to her boss, Nina, via her now tragically deceased husband, Detective James Nathan West.

[481] Learn more about Sweetie Ward in the section entitled "Don't Know Much About History."

The university arranged a campus screening that proved so popular it soon grew into the full-fledged festival that we know and love today. The biggest of its kind for hundreds of miles around, PCIFF not only features art house gems like *Vicker Man—The David Vickers Buchanan Story*,[482] but local voices of independent cinema as well. The Port Charles Chamber of Commerce, in conjunction with PCU's Film Studies Department, sponsors a yearly contest for budding area talent called "What's Your Story?" The contest encourages local filmmakers to tell stories about their own Port Charles.

Recent entries have included Damian Spinelli's Daliesque Claymation account of the 2007 Metro Court Hotel hostage incident entitled *Hotel Hijinks* and Kristina Corinthos's searing documentary about the dangers of coffee consumption, *Wicked Brew*. Prizes include an internship with Aurora Media and an all-expense paid trip to Los Angeles to visit the set of Dillon Quartermaine's latest buzz-worthy project.

PORT CHARLES PICKLE FESTIVAL

If November rolls around and you find yourself yearning for a briny dip, you need not plunge into the lake with the Port Charles Polar Bears;[483] visit the Port Charles Pickle-palooza instead! It was inspired by the 1986 release of the relish that swept the nation, Pickle-Lila,[484] and its 2013 sequel, Pickle-Eddie.[485] Picklers the world over convene in the fairgrounds every November to hawk their goods, share tips, and find out what's new in the science of preserves. But you don't have to be a gherkin-lovin' granny, connoisseur of kimchi,

[482] Starring David Vickers Buchanan as himself. Prior to its screening at the PCIFF, *Vicker Man* was little seen. Critically drubbed, it was run out of theaters almost as soon as it premiered. In later years, though, *Vicker Man* has developed a cult following. Midnight showings swarmed by devoted fans, or "Vickies," are a regular occurrence at theaters across the country. One distinguished Vicky is Port Charles's own Monica Quartermaine. "An unsung gem," says Monica of the eyebrow-raising film. Every year at the PCIFF she hosts a screening and talk-back with cast and crew. "David Vickers himself has yet to attend, but I know I'll get him here one of these days. Perhaps if I offered to bankroll a sequel. . . ."

[483] First organized decades ago by former GH chief of staff Steve Hardy, who bragged that he could swim a mile in the lake's frigid waters and then perform a quadruple bypass without missing a (heart)beat.

[484] Lucy's note: I had to call Amsterdam ten times before Lila's daughter, Tracy, would finally pick up the phone—and another ten times to get her to comment! It's a peculiar quirk of her personality—not appreciating me, that is. Lila and I got along just fine. "I wasn't even in Port Charles when Monica and Sean Donely's scheming forced Mother to turn to pickling to save the family." Monica had embarked on a torrid affair with Sean, and then together they set out to steal the Quartermaine fortune—right before she tossed the family out of the house. "It was a different time," Monica sighs. "We were cheating on each other left and right." Edward and Lila were forced to lodge at Kelly's—but not for long. Lila and her trusty maid, Stella, perfected a secret family relish recipe and sprung it on the wide world—to instant acclaim! The Qs were back in business, but not back in their house. That wouldn't come to pass until Alan faked his death, pinned it on Sean, and blackmailed him into relinquishing their fortune. "Not one of my finer moments," Sean laments. As was their way, Alan and Monica fell back into bed. "Definitely one of *my* finer moments," Monica tells me.

[485] Lucy's note: Those rich but beleaguered Quartermaines fell on similarly troubled times nearly thirty years later, when Edward's death triggered a fight for control of ELQ. Tracy got pushed out—but not for long. "Inexplicably, Daddy's will left me nothing but a single jar of Pickle-lila." A sour turn of events, to be sure. "But there was gold in that relish." Tracy won her way back into the company when she reverse engineered Pickle-lila to discover its secret ingredient, redubbed it for her father, and rereleased it. A windfall was made and Tracy was back in business.

or pundit of all things pickled to join in the fun. You can stop to enjoy or shudder at the pickle-eating contest[486] or take part in the pickle flinging completion, for which Lulu

Spencer Falconeri set the record last year with a throw of 252 feet! Didn't I tell you that Port Charles has it all?

MOB-STACLE COURSE

Former police commissioner Mac Scorpio organized the first annual Mob-stacle Course in 2013 as a charity event to benefit the Port Charles Police Athletic League.[487] In its first year, the Mob-stacle was open only to current and former members of the PCPD.[488] But when local boosters Sonny Corinthos and Julian Jerome learned of its existence, they threw down the gauntlet, challenging the PD to loosen entrance criteria and direct monies raised to help fund youth leagues and after-school programs. Mac took up the challenge, pitting the PCPD against the best that Corinthos Coffee and Derek Wells Media[489] had to offer.[490] Teams and single

competitors from around the globe now flock to Port Charles to fight their way across a ten-mile course and through such deterrents as "The Coffee Haul Crawl," a timed event in which contestants have three minutes to unload a ton's worth of "coffee" before the Feds close in; "The Master of Snake-Eyes," in which contestants must roll two one hundred pound dice until they get double ones; and "The Concealed Carry," in which contestants must guess the amount of secreted weight carried by their teammates. Friends, this course is not for the faint of heart, nor for the muddy of mind.

> *. . . this course is not for the faint of heart . . .*

[486] Two-time Palme d'Pickle winner Alexis Davis has recently faced stiff competition from Bradley Cooper.

[487] Lucy's note: Or was it to show *off* for Felicia Jones and show *up* her ex-husband, WSB spy chief Frisco? It was in 2013 that Frisco made one of his surprise drop-ins to Port Charles to win back the lady of his heart, but in the end it was Mac who got the girl. Maybe it was seeing him shirtless and pushing and pulling and hoisting and hucking that helped Felicia make up her notoriously fickle mind.

[488] Mac won the race, followed close behind by Detective Dante Falconeri. Mother Olivia and wife Lulu waited at the finish line with baked ziti for all and a banner congratulating those who completed the harrowing course. "I was so embarrassed," Dante claims. His smile tells a different story.

[489] Purchasers Drew Cain and Sam Morgan have since re-branded Julian's former company "Aurora Media."

[490] The PD and its adversaries have traded wins over the years. Julian Jerome, "Magic" Milo Giambetti, and Detective Nathan West have all won bragging rights.

hen you come to Port Charles you better come hungry! Your mouth will water and your cup runneth over at the abundance of dining options. Sample fine fare from surf to turf, exceptional locally sourced entrees, and a world's worth of international[491] cuisine. Whether you're looking for a quick bite, a family-style meal, or an upscale dining establishment, Port Charles has a little something for everybody. What are you hungry for?

KELLY'S DINER[492]

Kelly's is the ultimate greasy spoon, that also happens to rent rooms upstairs. Known originally for Paddy and Rose Kelly's hearty Irish breakfasts, Kelly's developed a second-round reputation courtesy of its next owner, Ruby Anderson. Her "Famous Chili" satisfies famished parents the county over as the younger set clambers for chocolate pancakes. But don't take my word for it! Just read the reviews:

Says Lulu F, "This is where the discomfited come for comfort eats. Kelly's hash browns are the cure all for almost anything. I admit to having a sentimental attachment to the place. Ruby and my aunt Bobbie charted my height on the wall at the second-floor landing. Every now and then my dad and I would meet at Kelly's for coffee before opening up the Haunted Star, and every now and then I'd catch him at the second-floor landing with a glint in his eye. So much for tough-guy Luke Spencer."

But, counters Spencer C, "Pedestrian fare and rude service. I asked for cashew milk in my hot chocolate and received a laugh and a pat on my head. HARD PASS."

Says Liz W, "I used to work at Kelly's, so I may be a bit biased. Among their many delicacies is a strawberry milkshake that tastes as though it was pureed right off the vine. Ask for yours with a shot of chocolate sauce to really tingle the taste buds."

Says Heather W, "Get the BLT."

This is where the discomfited come for comfort eats

---

[491] Offers Shep C, "Or intergalactic!"
[492] 324 Wharf Street

METRO COURT RESTAURANT[493]

This chic and sophisticated martini bar and restaurant located at the top of the Metro Court Hotel, is owned and operated by Carly Corinthos and Olivia Falconeri-Quartermaine. The lounge has an inviting private space that can accommodate large private parties, as well as road-weary travelers looking for a nightcap, and a terrace that opens to the Port Charles skyline. The menu is New American fare, with a Continental twist. On Tuesdays the lounge holds a Manager's Reception from 5–7 p.m. with complimentary hors d'oeuvres and drinks for hotel guests.

Says Drew C, "Not only did I once serve drinks here, I created a secret menu of cocktails that might help you 'forget' who you are for a while, too."

Says Jasper J, "Whenever I'm in town, I like to meet friends at the Metro Court. Its views and people watching can't be beat. Be sure to stop by on lobster night. A snapshot of your teenaged daughter in a bib is worth the price of dinner alone!"

Says Josslyn J, "When I was little, I always asked for a Mary Poppins instead of a Shirley Temple, so they went ahead and put it on the menu. That's the kind of place the Metro Court is; they'll take care of what you need and put it in writing."

POZZULO'S FINE ITALIAN EATERY[494]

Owned by Sonny Corinthos, Pozzulo's is a "legitimate" establishment,[495] so the only shoot-out you're liable to take part in is on the *Big Buck Hunter* in the back room. Billed as serving classic Italian fare and artisanal pizzas, Pozzulo's has become the go-to spot for first dates and last dates alike. At Pozzulo's, be prepared to dine family style, as most dishes are meant to be shared.

Says Dante F, "The best sweet potato gnocchi, just like my grandma used to make in Brooklyn."[496]

Says Mac S, "Delicious Italian cuisine, only somewhat detracted from by the likelihood of criminal activity going on in the kitchen."

Says Franco, "The best place for a first date, because they don't have a kids menu. So as much as you might love your date's kiddos, they can't come along. Also, Sonny is always thrilled to see you."

> *The best place for a first date, because they don't have a kids menu*

---

[493] 1470 Quartz Lane
[494] 820 South Clinton Avenue
[495] Says Corinthos family lawyer Diane Miller, "Naturally."
[496] Says Olivia F-Q, "Probably because he yoinked it from her."

CHARLIE'S PUB [497]

Owned by Julian Jerome, Charlie's Gastro Pub is an up-and-coming spot for brunch. Get there early for your cup of Corinthos coffee and famous avocado toast; on weekends, tables go fast. Come afternoons, the brunch crowd thins out, replaced by those seeking small-batch craft beers to swig while enjoying the Woodchucks play the Red Wings on WXPC. Located in the historic Charles Street District, Charlie's is well situated for a quick bite before a show at the nearby Amanda Barrington Center for the Arts.

Says Lucas J, "I love their pre-fixe menu themed to whatever is happening at the Barrington at that moment. My favorite was the 'My Fair Lady-Fingers' dessert special."

Says Nina R, "When I was in a coma for all those years, the one meal I dreamed of was a chicken potpie. The kind with the flaky crust and the gooey, creamy center? My dreams finally came true when I lobbied Julian into putting one on the menu."

Says Kevin C, "I appreciate that they have a variety of local microbrews on tap. One can only drink so much water-flavored beer."

When I was in a coma . . . the one meal I dreamed of was a chicken potpie

[497] 298 Elm Street

NOODLE BUDDHA[498]

Located in the Asian Quarter, Noodle Buddha is known for its dual menus: one features standard Chinese fare, atypically prepared; the other features Korean-Italian fusion that has all the Port Charles foodies buzzing. Ingredients favor ramen, and the design leans toward small sharable plates. Come on Sunday and try their all-you-can-eat dim sum brunch.

Says Sam M, "My favorite restaurant bar none, and not just because they host a mean wedding. No one can beat their Chicken Lo Mein, the perfect balm for a rough day, or year. My son Danny is so fluent with chopsticks he teaches the kids at school."

Says Cameron W, "I love this place because they always give me extra hot sauce to I take home to stockpile for the spiking of Spencer's food. He deserves it."

Says Robin S-D, "When I was a kid, my dad and I used to throw down for dumpling-eating contests here once a month. We still hold the record of twenty-six dumplings in three minutes!"

FLOATING RIB[499]

Formerly Jake's Bar, the Floating Rib is Port Charles's premiere rib joint, pool hall, karaoke bar, and fight scene. The BBQ sauce here is said to be so good you're liable to slap your mother. Bring a bib—the Rib is usually so jammed at lunch they run out by dinnertime.

Says Damian S, "It is said that when I imbibe too much I am known to exercise my vocal cords.[500] Thank goodness I limit my consumption to the Rib. The crowds are friendly and the critics kind."

Says Patrick D, "Late at night you're liable to run into a big group of doctors and nurses coming off a long shift. If it's quiet, it's because we're famished and sour mouths are full."

Says Epiphany J, "The jukebox is mine. And don't come for me at air hockey."

Says Kristina C, "The only lesbian party worth going to is on Thursday nights at the Rib."

Valerie S agrees: "One night at the Butch Brisket changed my life."

The BBQ sauce here is said to be so good you're liable to slap your mother

---

[498] 65 Mott Street
[499] 345 Portside Road
[500] Says Maxie J-W, "He knows all the folk songs from the *Lord of the Rings*—in English and Elvish!"

WHERE TO

While the act of shopping has always aligned my chakras and opened my third eye, I understand there are some folks who answer to a calling even higher than a sale at Wyndham's. Here are a few spots that can offer religion and occasionally a timely visit from a loved one long thought lost—and I am not talking about the Resurrection.

. . . a school that provided religious education for many of Port Charles's good and not-so-good Catholics . . .

WORSHIP

ST. TIMOTHY'S CHURCH[501]

Currently officiated by Father Coates,[502] this church was a peaceful spot—until Brenda Barrett[503] escaped captivity from arms dealer Luis Alcazar's yacht. She sent word to Sonny Corinthos to meet her at the spot where they were once to be married. Unbeknownst to Brenda, Sonny's enemies were lying in wait. No sooner had he locked eyes with Brenda than he was gunned down.[504] Aside from that it's really a lovely church!

MOUNT HEBRON CHURCH[505]

Located in the Charles Street neighborhood, this church is notable as having been the base of operations for state assemblyman and community organizer Bradley Ward—until his disappearance in 1974.[506]

QUEEN OF ANGELS CHURCH[507]

Port Charles's oldest Catholic Church dates back to the early nineteenth century. Its vast campus includes a school that provided religious education for many of Port Charles's good and not-so-good Catholics, including the late Morgan Corinthos.[508]

---

[501] 1123 North Main Street

[502] One notable former officiant was Father Mateo Ruiz, twin to a somewhat less godly brother, gangster Manny Ruiz.

[503] Editor's note: Believed perished in a car accident caused by her unhinged mother, Veronica

[504] Lucy's note: Never fear, it was a fake out! Sonny survived. Alcazar, alas, would not.

[505] 124 Elm Street

[506] Editor's note: Bradley Ward's fate was the subject of fevered speculation for twenty years. Had he taken off with a mistress? Gone on the lam to avoid prosecution for some shameful crime? Only his mother, activist and singer Mary Mae Ward, knew his true whereabouts—six feet under the rose garden of her old home, the house Luke and Laura Spencer moved into upon their return to Port Charles in 1993! The discovery of Bradley's body and subsequent autopsy kicked off a mystery that would stretch from World War II to the present-day, and cause ripple effects from humble Charles Street to City Hall and all the way to the manicured lawns of the Quartermaine estate. When the truth was finally out, Bradley was revealed to be Mary Mae's son by Edward Quartermaine! His murder was the result of his opposition to the money-grubbing plans of Edward's business associates many years prior. "When we learned that Bradley's son Justus was our cousin, we welcomed him into the family with open arms," says Ned Quartermaine. "Yeah," tsks Monica, "and a knife in the back." "That's how you know they love you," says Lucy. "If they hurt you, it's because they care."

[507] 600 Courtland Place

[508] Editor's note: Died in 2016 as the result of a car bomb believed intended for Julian Jerome, mob boss and former media magnate turned humble bar owner.

GENERAL HOSPITAL CHAPEL[509]

Located on the second floor near the entrance to the Stone Cates Memorial AIDS Wing, this is the spot where many a Port Charles resident has prayed to a higher power to make sure their child/parent/newly discovered adult child/love makes it out of a surgery and/or coma alive.

ST. ANNE'S CEMETERY[510]

The final resting place for many of Port Charles's most prominent residents, St. Anne's is the location of the Jerome family crypt, where Oliva Jerome[511] was supposedly buried.

THE ZEN CENTER[512]

Located in the Asian Quarter, here is a spot that not enough residents take advantage of. The ornate shrine has a healing Buddha, who has been said to give a lifetime of good luck to those who truly believe in peace and harmony.[513] Just remember to take your shoes off before you enter.

BROTHERHOOD SYNAGOGUE OF PORT CHARLES[514]

Throws the best Hanukkah parties in town.[515] This also is the spot where my former fling Jake Meyer had his bar mitzvah and where the notorious Hayden Barnes[516] attends High Holiday services when she is in town.

---

[509] 6065 Central Avenue

[510] 6 Talmadge Street

[511] Lucy's note: How Olivia "Liv" Jerome survived being shot in open court by her brother, Julian, is something I'm very curious to find out. Maybe survival is just a Jerome family trait. Brother Julian turned up very much alive two decades after his rival/my good friend Duke Lavery shot him "to death" in 1990; sister Ava survived plunging off a bridge "to her death" after escaping Pentonville Prison, then even more improbably survived a *very* bad black dye job as she pretended to be her own look-alike, Brooklynite Denise DiMuccio. The only Jerome I know whose death *did* take was head of the family, Victor. He fell in love with me, the dear, and when I wouldn't reciprocate his affection, he swallowed a necklace he'd bought for me, choked on it, and keeled over. I suppose if you've gotta go, you can do worse than death by diamonds.

[512] 7203 West 3rd Street

[513] Liv Jerome phoned from her digs in the D'Archam Asylum to comment, "Ha! In Port Charles? Even the dead get no peace!"

[514] 898 Albany Avenue

[515] Lucy's note: I'm told to pass on advice to watch out for Rabbi Cohen, possessor of "crazy good" dreidel skills.

[516] Hayden Barnes, half sister to Elizabeth Webber on dad Jeff's side, stood to inherit a great deal of money from her wealthy adoptive dad—until he turned out to be a deadbeat on par with Bernie Madoff. A failed romance with curmudgeonly-but-cute Dr. Hamilton Finn sent Hayden packing for parts unknown in 2017.

WHERE TO DITCH THE KIDS

For those of you who have children of the flesh and blood,[517] I've asked everyone's favorite pint-sized romantic to weigh in with his thoughts. Take it away, Spencer Cassadine![518]

Most of us kids in town have been through a lot. Surely more than our counterparts in New York and LA. For instance, my mother died[519] of a plague right after I was born;[520] then I had it, and so did my father,[521] but luckily we survived. I got kidnapped for a while, but then I went home with my dad and my new[522] mom, but then she died.[523] And that was all before I could talk.[524] Us kids can get a little stressed out in Port Charles, so here are some recommendations for relaxation designed specifically for kids, coming at you from me and my pals Cameron Spencer[525] and Emma Drake.

[517] Lucy's note: As opposed to the feathered variety. I have both!

[518] Spencer's parents are Nikolas Cassadine and Courtney Matthews.

[519] Lucy's note: This got dark very fast.

[520] Editor's note: As well as Jasper Jacks, who at the time was also a candidate for Spencer's paternity.

[521] Editor's note: Emily Quartermaine

[522] Editor's note: Murdered by the Text Message Killer

[523] Sighs Laura C, "Things got even loonier after that."

[524] Spencer further comments, "More of a forced acquaintance than a pal."

VOLONINO'S GYM[525]

Says Emma, "If you're feeling like you have a lot of energy after a long car ride, drop into Volonino's. This gym is mainly for boxing, so if fencing[526] or squash[527] is your thing,[528] you'll have to go elsewhere. Volonino's is owned by my mom's friend Sonny,[529] and he trains here every day. "At Volonino's we offer a ton of classes just for kids," says Sonny. "Everything from karate to kickboxing." The better to fight off would-be kidnappers.

LILA'S KIDS[530]

Says Cameron, "If you're in Port Charles for the summer, come to Lila's Kids Day Camp! Refine your archery skills, make beaded bracelets, and learn to hack computers with counselor Damian Spinelli! There are lots of security cameras (now),[531] if your parents are worried about that kind of thing. Campers become part of a community that doesn't have shoot-outs and, as our camp's namesake Lila Quartermaine said, "forge friendships that span generations."

CAMP SHOWBIZ[532]

Says Spencer, "Sure, you *could* go to Lila's Kids, where you *might* meet someone who can form a coherent thought. It's *possible* you could have some fun doing the underwater basket weaving when you're not in the infirmary coughing up a lung from the lousy food. Or you could learn to be a star! Camp Showbiz is the hottest acting school this side of Stage Door! At Camp Showbiz the counselors are made up of the finest swings and backup dancers regional theater has to offer! And we don't limit ourselves to improving games and children's theater; a couple years ago I was set to perform *Richard III*[533] before a crowd that I'm told included real agents!"

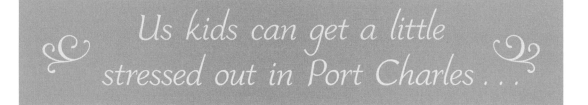

Us kids can get a little stressed out in Port Charles...

[525] 152 Broadway

[526] Says Spencer C, "Swordplay is definitely my thing. En garde, Cameron!"

[527] Says Spencer C, "Yellow vegetables are definitely not my thing."

[528] Says Cameron W, "She's talking about the SPORT."

[529] Brags Spencer C, "He's MY uncle."

[530] Elm Park.

[531] Lucy's note: There was an unfortunate incident one summer, but everyone is okay!

[532] Classes held at the Amanda Barrington Center; performances held in public spaces across Port Charles.

[533] Adds Spencer C, "And then my crazy uncle Valentin tried to kidnap me. But then my good uncle Sonny saved me!"

GENERAL HOSPITAL CARNIVAL

Says Emma, "Sometime they have a carnival in the parking lot of the hospital, complete with ball tosses, cotton candy, Ferris wheels, and your parents' friends dressed as clowns.[534] Just stay close to your parents so you don't get caught in a tight spot.[535]

SCAVENGER HUNT

Says Emma, "If these tour ideas are *still* leaving your kids as bored as I was the time my dad tried to explain how everyone in Port Charles is connected,[536] Cameron and I created a game for you all to enjoy.[537] Really, Port Charles is a great place to organize a scavenger hunt.[538] This game is appropriate for kids of all ages! Grab your favorite second cousin or father you thought was dead but who returned with a new face and let's begin!"

"Here is a list of things players should be able to find in the different neighborhoods of Port Charles. You get two hours to try to find one of each."

1. Any piece of Aztec treasure
2. Lumina crystal
3. Chupacabra
4. Dragon bone
5. A draft of Lila Quartermaine's memoirs
6. Something crimson
7. A copy of P. K. Sinclair's book *The Alpine Express*, or a copy of Molly Lansing-Davis's book *Love in Maine*

"The first team to gather all of the items wins!" Says Spencer, "My aunt Lulu says we're all winners if we have fun, but clearly she's never won anything in her life. So, she has to say that."

Port Charles is a great place to organize a scavenger hunt

[534] Says Emma S-D, "Hi Spinelli!"
[535] Lucy's note: Like a shoot-out, or Edward Quartermaine playing real-life bumper cars with his Mercedes.
[536] Asks Emma S-D, "How can so many kids have begun life as frozen embryos?"
[537] Says Spencer C, "This game is also suitable for adults who enjoy childish things, which is most of Port Charles."
[538] Says Cameron W, "The hospital is the best place for a scavenger hunt, but my mom vetoed it when she saw one of our tasks was to find a bedpan and put it to good use.

For all its dazzling qualities, Port Charles is in some ways like any other midsize American city. You can't take your own well-being for granted. Look both ways when you cross the street.[539] Don't let that tickle in the back of your throat[540] go unaddressed. And steer clear of known mob haunts.[541] But the sad, cosmological fact is that we're no more in control of our own lives than we are in control of anyone else's.[542] Fate steps in when we least expect it, and with it stubbed toes and sniffly noses.[543] And when the unexpected strikes, you're in no better place to receive treatment than Port Charles—provided you know where to go. So pay close attention to the information in these pages, people![544]

MERCY HOSPITAL[545]

Do not go to Mercy. Do not visit friends or family who are admitted to Mercy. Do not allow an ambulance to take you to Mercy. Do not accept assistance from any medical professional who works at Mercy, even if you are shot and bleeding in the street. Wait for someone else to come. Operate on yourself if you must. Avoid the butchers at Mercy Hospital at all costs. If for some wretched reason you do find yourself admitted to Mercy, do not bother to pray for salvation or make peace with your god. You are already dead.

GENERAL HOSPITAL INFO[546]

People make the pilgrimage to Port Charles for loads of reasons—but one of the biggest is our world-renowned hospital. And while I'm just the woman to tell you where in town to buy the best pair of shoes,[547] or the best place to meet for a confidential canoodle,[548] I thought I'd let a professional give you the skinny on what put this place on the map:

---

[539] Editor's note: And sometimes repeat. Especially if you're crossing Route 31 at any point in its entire length. More accidents occur on Route 31 than on any other stretch in the city.

[540] Editor's note: In Port Charles, it's unlikely that a simple antibiotic will suffice.

[541] Editor's note: Self-explanatory.

[542] Says Ned Q, "I can hear Grandfather grumbling from his grave."

[543] Editor's note: As will more traumatic injuries and ailments. Some can be avoided altogether simply by avoiding certain tricky situations common to Port Charles. See the guidelines set forth in the PCPD's handy pamphlet, *A Smart Tourist Is a Safe Tourist: Surviving a Visit to Port Charles.*

[544] Editor's note: Your life may depend upon it.

[545] Address provided against Lucy's wishes: 500 Atlantic Avenue.

[546] 6065 Central Avenue

[547] Wyndham's Department Store, located at 620 North Main Street.

[548] Any dock will do.

General Hospital. Without further ado, here's my girl, GH head nurse Epiphany Johnson.

When I first took over as head nurse from Audrey Hardy over a decade ago, I was struck by many things at this hospital: the fine[549] doctors, the terrible cafeteria food,[550] and the fact that this place seems to be a lightning rod for cases that make *The X-Files* look tame. It's no wonder the *New York Journal of Medicine* often leaves room in each issue for a case study[551] from our staff.

LASSA FEVER

In the winter of 1979, Port Charles was hit by an epidemic of Lassa fever. General Hospital was placed under quarantine by the Bureau of Disease Control. When you have that many people cooped up with nowhere to go, mouths get to flapping, secrets start flying, and tempers and passions burn hotter than Lee Baldwin's virus-induced fever! Monica was itching[552] to jump Rick Webber's bones, later telling me she almost tattooed her wrist with the phrase, "I'm married to Alan, I do love Alan!" And the biggest bonfire of all: Jeff Webber discovered his father is none other than Chief Steve Hardy himself! The virus was ultimately contained with a mixture of drugs, isolation, and Mother Nature doing her good work, winnowing the herd. However, the bombshells that got dropped went kaboom for a long time to come.

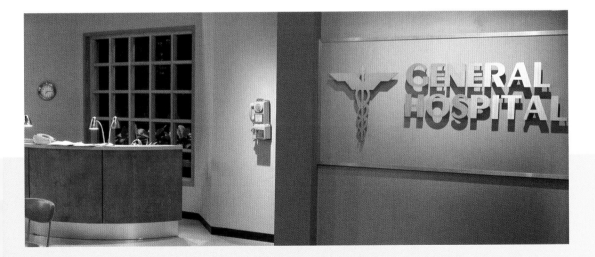

---

[549] Confides Epiphany, "Fine to operate and fine to look at."
[550] Editor's note: As of this fall, the catering staff from the Metro Court is assuming control of food services at General Hospital.
[551] Editor's note: In each case study that is being shared, doctor/patient confidentiality was waived by all referenced individuals.
[552] Lucy's note: Not from the Lassa fever, mind you. . . .

B.J.'S HEART

I stop and say a prayer whenever I pass the wood carving in the children's ward. It's of a little heart with the initials "BJJ" on the inside. This place has been built, razed, rebuilt, exploded, and rebuilt again—but that carving has somehow remained. Though I had to come on board at GH, I feel like I lived the saga of B. J. Jones's death just the same. In May of 1994, that sweet girl, the beloved daughter of Tony and Bobbie Jones, was left brain-dead after her school van was hit by a drunk driver. Tony made the unbearable decision to donate B.J.'s heart to his niece Maxie, then slowly wasting away of Kawasaki's syndrome as she awaited the only thing that would save her life: a compatible heart for transplant. After the surgery, Dr. Jones lay his head on Maxie's chest and listened to the beat of his daughter's heart and, oh here I go crying again.[553] When this was happening, a local crew from the KRPC radio station happened to be recording a story about pediatric nurses. The family has given us permission to print the transcript of a conversation depicted on the show that displays our humanity, and our hospital, at its best:

Frisco (Maxie's father, Tony's brother): Tony, I've been looking all over for you. I got some news. You're not gonna believe this. We got a heart for Maxie. There was a child that was in an accident. And she was just brought into the ER. And, well, the most amazing part is that they've tested her and . . . the type matches. The blood matches. The tissue matches. They're prepping her for a transplant right now. We got our miracle.

Tony: Yes, you did.

Frisco: I know. I mean, I can't stop thinking of those parents of the child.

Tony: The heart for Maxie is B.J.'s. The school van crashed and overturned, and B.J. was pinned. And she had massive head trauma. And they put her on a ventilator when they brought her into the ER. But she was essentially brain-dead when she got there. And there's not any chance. So when I found out that Maxie carried the small "P" factor, I had myself and B.J. tested. And it's lucky that I did, because B.J. carried the small "P" factor, so she's the same as Maxie. I told Monica to go ahead.

Frisco: Thank you. Thank you. I'm so sorry.

LUCY'S SURROGACY

Now she might cut this out, but "selfless" is not the first word that comes to mind when asked to describe Ms. Lucy Coe. This case proved that extraordinary acts of kindness can come from the most unexpected of places. Lucy took a little respite from Port Charles but came back right quick and went looking for her ex, Scott Baldwin. But he'd since moved on with Dominique Stanton.[554]

---

[553] Says Maxie J-W: "I think about B.J. always. No matter what, I'll never have another heart replacement because I'm living life for the both of us."

[554] Lucy's note: I don't believe in censorship—unless it's the lyrics to a few Blackie Parish tunes; they're just so awful. Carrying Dominque's baby was one of those moments in which doing the right thing just sort of happens naturally. And Serena was the end result, so I'd say the whole world was the winner.

Dominique had been diagnosed with terminal cancer, and it appeared that her dream of having a baby with Scott would die with her. While I hear Scott was reluctant to trust her, Dominique saw a kinder, gentler Lucy and convinced Scott to allow Lucy to be the surrogate mother to their child. After Dominique died, Lucy gave birth to their daughter, Serena, in a cabin during a blizzard.

STONE CATES'S BATTLE WITH HIV

Stone Cates was dead and buried by the time I started at GH. But I know from those who loved him that his fire burned bright. Stone was just a kid, really, hardly even twenty when he came down with what he thought was a bad flu. Although he'd been tested for HIV and received a negative result before, this time the test came back positive. The boy was devastated and couldn't bring himself to tell his girlfriend, our own Robin Scorpio. After being shot in the crossfire of one of the million attempts on his friend Sonny Corinthos's life, some of Stone's blood got on Robin. He did his best to wipe it off, but then he panicked and took off. Robin found him at the Rendezvous Motel. Stone tearfully told Robin he'd tested HIV positive. His case file reveals he was infected by a former girlfriend who had also been an intravenous drug user.

Back at the hospital, Robin first tested negative—but that was just the first of several. This was back in the day that a test wasn't proved reliably right at first. If you thought you'd been exposed you'd have to go on for another year; year and a half to be absolutely sure. Soon Stone's HIV developed into full-blown AIDS. Dr. Alan Quartermaine started Stone on experimental drug therapy, but only so much could be done to treat Stone's advanced case.

As Stone grew weaker his eyesight began to fail. One of the attending doctors told me that on the day of his death Stone told Robin to stand near the light of the window . . . and in that second something changed. Stone received a moment of grace. He saw the woman he loved with his own eyes right before he passed. Stone's battle with AIDS changed everyone in this town and transformed General Hospital into a leading center for cutting-edge HIV and AIDS research. When she heard I was writing this section of the book, Dr. Monica Quartermaine asked to contribute.

Says Monica, "I recently read a book about decluttering, and while attempting to organize the belongings of the dozens of people who have lived in this house at one time or another, I came across a box labeled, ONLY IMPORTANT TO THOSE WHO CARE. In this box were the diaries of my late-husband, Alan Quartermaine. They smelled just like him, a mix of leather, wool, and common sense.[555] When Lucy said she was putting this book together about important people and places in Port Charles, I thought some of his entries might be appropriate. Except for some of his musings about certain women. No one needs to see that.

> *. . . General Hospital is a leading center for cutting-edge HIV and AIDS research*

[555] Sniffles Lucy, "He used up all his common sense for his practice. In his private life, the big galoot wasn't too canny. He might believe anyone who claimed to be a relative."

DIARY
OF
ALAN QUARTERMAINE

From the diary of

Alan Quartermaine

1994

Today was one of those days they warn you about in medical school, where the personal and professional are so intertwined you find it hard to breathe. I've known Robin Scorpio since she was a little girl. She used to beat me at cards all the time. When Dr. Collins asked me to consult on an HIV case, I had no idea the patient was her boyfriend, Stone Cates. When Stone asked me if his status would get out and people would treat him like a freak, I saw her squeeze his hand the way Monica has squeezed mine through so many trials that were not nearly so bleak. As I told Stone that none of us would divulge his medical condition without his consent, I couldn't stop thinking about the young lady next to him. Was she exposed? This is one round of poker I desperately pray she wins.

1995

Stone came into my office this afternoon with the first smile he had in months. His report showed his retina damage had slowed considerably. While he was full of hope at this development I was in possession of lab results that belied his optimism. Stone's T cell count was down to 53. When he asked whether his count could increase I so wanted to tell him yes. But some facts sap hope. I was impressed with his research into protease inhibitors. He'd found research on how beneficial these drugs might be. What a mind that boy has, what a doctor he could be someday. If only there were a someday. His liver tests are just too high. Even if we could achieve the impossible and place him on a drug trial, it is doubtful he could even survive the first round of treatment. Sometimes hope is not a thing with feathers. Not even close.

Monica's Breast Cancer

My grandfather had a quote that I often reflect on when assisting difficult surgeries: "Scars are tattoos with better stories." Grandpa's wisdom fits right into the next, which happens to involve none other than our chief of staff herself, Monica Quartermaine. After experiencing discomfort in her breasts, Monica had finally went in for a mammogram at GH. The results showed a lump in her right breast. A biopsy revealed breast cancer. She opted to receive treatment in Arizona,[556] had a mastectomy, and ultimately went into remission. But the feelings of insecurity resulting from that surgery caused her to rebuff Alan, putting a terrible strain on their marriage. Monica pushed through, and I know that the scar from her mastectomy reminds her every day to live life to its fullest.

"Scars are tattoos with better stories"

Grandpa's wisdom

[556] Editor's note: It was at the clinic in Arizona that Monica met Paige Bowen, whose untimely death brought her daughter, Emily, into our lives.

Monkey Virus

In 2006, Luke Spencer did what all absentee dads do best: bring their child a highly unsuitable gift to make up for not being there. In this case, Luke returned to Port Charles with two presents: a rescued chimp for his daughter, Lulu, and a contagious strain of viral encephalitis virus that bore a terrifyingly high mortality rate.

Another runner-up in the disappearing dad pageant, the presumed dead Robert Scorpio, followed Luke to town and was horrified when he observed the citizens of Port Charles displaying symptoms of the deadly disease. While breaking into hospital records to gather information on the disease, Robert was discovered by his daughter Robin—who unleashed holy hell on her father for his many years of absence. Robert told her he'd been forced into the undercover spy game before a change of leadership within the WSB finally released him from his contract. I'll never forget watching friends sick with the virus admitted to the hospital one by one: Sonny, Nikolas, Sam, Skye, Lulu, and so many others.

Robert and Robin teamed up to trace the origin of the virus, quickly ruling out Lulu's chimp . . . but homing in on Luke Spencer himself, who turned out to not only be Patient Zero, but also the source of an antidote. Despite the danger to his own health, he agreed to donate blood that would be used to develop the antidote—but synthesizing the cure took time, and only so much could be made.

But the virus claimed its victims. Tony Jones was one of the few doctors to never get on my bad side . . . much. I'll always remember him encouraging his son Lucas[557] to embrace and be proud of his identity as a gay man. Just before he left this earth, Tony told his family that B.J. was with him and he was dying a happy man. Tony's death meant that another patient could be saved by his share of the antidote.

The death toll from the virus soon rose faster than Tracy Quartermaine's hair at the sound of a Brooklyn accent, taking the life of Sam McCall's brothers Danny and Courtney Jacks. In Courtney's case, Dr. Drake published[558] a case study on how he was able to save her unborn baby by administering a Caesarian section right before she died. The whole ordeal ended with everyone's favorite nondoctors, Carly Corinthos and Jason Morgan, locating larger quantities of the antidote and saving everyone—that is, everyone who lived that long.[559]

---

[557] Editor's note: Although Lucas Jones considered Tony Jones to be his father, it has recently been revealed that his biological father is Julian Jerome.

[558] *New England Journal of Medicine* 2007 case study, "Not Monkeying Around."

[559] Holly Sutton—who was intimately involved in the creation of the virus—also returned to Port Charles, demanding millions in exchange for providing the antidote. People who knew her say she barely resembled the Holly they'd once loved. She didn't get her money—just a mess of legal trouble.

Biotoxin Spheres

Working in an emergency room, it seems like the things that go wrong always stay with you the most. I'll never forget in 2009 when the biotoxin ordeal began. Things started going wrong during an operation Monica was performing. After her patient began bleeding out, Monica fainted. We soon discovered that the patient on the table had been carrying classified material WITHIN HIS BODY—that classified material being spherical containers of a deadly biotoxin. The poison became airborne when Earl was opened up in surgery. My team was quickly overcome with the deadly poison. Matt Drake, Monica, and Elizabeth Webber were in critical condition. Andy Archer, a very fine anesthesiologist, was the first to die. Others followed.

The toxin traveled through the hospital's ventilation system, and more succumbed. Once again, the hospital was put under quarantine. Trevor Lansing was among the victims. Lansing revealed he was in possession of a missing sphere of biotoxin. On the hospital rooftop, Trevor and Sam struggled for the vial. Badass Sam won out and Trevor plummeted to his death. Jason managed to nab the sphere of poison before it smashed on the sidewalk and killed us all.

Tainted Water Supply

A common theme among our hospital's famous cases is the man-made crisis that only one person can solve. In 2012, Jerry Jacks warned folks in town that a "deadly pathogen" had been put into their tap water. The FBI appointed hottie investigator John McBain to be its field rep during the crisis. Jerry agreed to hand over the antidote in exchange for a mere $88,111,000.00! Jerry's brother, Jax, and Sam realized such a specific number had to be a clue to Jerry's intentions, and maybe a way to defeat him.[560] Llanview, PA, publisher Todd Manning met with four of the wealthiest citizens of Port Charles—Carly and Sonny Corinthos, Johnny Zacchara, and Tracy Quartermaine—to ask them to pay their share of Jerry's demand in exchange for the cure. Nothing in this town is that easy. Jerry kidnapped Alexis and took off on his boat. The whole nightmare reached its end when Jerry's boat blew up and he was presumed dead.[561] Dante and Lulu were able to grab the anti-pathogen before it was destroyed, and they rushed it to us at the hospital. My team delivered the counteragent, but not before the Quartermaine family's beloved cook, Cook (Cook Two's predecessor), died of the fever. Funny, I never did get to see her face. . . .

---

[560] Adds Epiphany, "I and about a thousand other people played those numbers in the lottery—to no avail."
[561] Lucy's note: Which means nothing in this town.

Toxoplasmosis

People often ask me why I am not an animal person. I'll admire them from afar, but the following case is the only answer I need. Sam Morgan gave birth to her second child in not the most sterile of environments—in a dirty, snowy ditch. She was not out in the woods trying to re-create her own version of WILD; she'd been kidnapped by her loco aunt Olivia (Jerome, not Falconeri). Jason (aka the man now known as Drew Cain) tracked her down and delivered Emily Scout Morgan right there on the ground.

You might be forgiven for thinking they'd earned some peace. Friends, this is Port Charles. At the hospital, Sam had visions she was being stalked by Sonny Corinthos. Some people whispered she might have a brain tumor, but it was soon discovered her hallucinations were the result of a nasty case of toxoplasmosis—which is usually caused by coming into contact with the, ahem, leavings of certain wild animals. Although Sam's case was treated, it wasn't before she'd shot Sonny Corinthos and left him to die in a deep hole. He survived, but I doubt either family will be in the market for a Christmas kitten anytime soon.

Due to the fact that the hospital has been subject to numerous catastrophes and renovations over the years, the actual layout has changed numerous times. But I can share with you the parts of the hospital that are named after local heroes:

Dominique Baldwin
PEDIATRIC AIDS CENTER:

After his wife's death in 1993, SCOTT BALDWIN donates some of his inheritance money to assist in funding GH's Pediatric AIDS Center in her name.

Steve Hardy
MEMORIAL LIBRARY:

After Dr. Hardy's death in 1996, General Hospital dedicates a memorial library on the second floor in his honor.

Stone Cates
MEMORIAL AIDS WING:

In 1996, SONNY CORINTHOS donates the money inherited to him from his LATE WIFE, to fund an entire AIDS wing in honor of Stone.

Michael Corinthos III
PEDIATRIC HEAD TRAUMA CENTER:

In 2009, CARLY JACKS funds the Michael Corinthos III Pediatric Head Trauma unit on the fourth floor, in honor of her son Michael, who fell into a coma after being shot in the head.

The Nurses Ball

Of my many[562] accomplishments, the General Hospital Nurses Ball ranks right up at the top of a list of the most impactful.[563] It was in 1994 that the Nurses Ball came into[564] being[565] as a fund-raiser to benefit research into the treatment and cure for HIV and AIDS. By then the specter of AIDS had long since swept the country, but it was soon to hit home in ways my friends and I could not have prepared for: the diagnoses of Stone Cates and Robin Scorpio. Though Stone would succumb to his condition, Robin has not; indeed, today her condition is chronic and manageable, not the death sentence it once was.

Doctors and researchers at GH have done their part to contribute to the battles won over HIV and AIDS—and they did them with funding raised in part by the efforts of everyone who threw together to put on a yearly party the likes of which Port Charles had never seen before and hasn't seen since. Since the Nurses Ball and its red carpet provide the international press corps with an annual who's

---

[562] Lucy's note: Many, many, many . . .
[563] Lucy's note: Along with bearing a daughter and my Fragrance Fellows "Fragrance of the Decade" win in 1994—six years before the decade was over!
[564] Editor's note: At the suggestion of Damian Smith.
[565] Lucy's note: Details!

who of Port Charles luminaries, I thought it would be fun to reflect on some of its highlights in years past. Joining me to provide his own youthful take on the Nurses Ball through the years is one of its more recent headliners, my friend and theater buff, Little Lord Spencer Cassadine.

Says Spencer, "Greetings, ladies and gentlemen! I was most intrigued when Ms. Coe asked me to review videos[566] of balls past. Could any performance hold a candle to my own? Let us find out. If you have a screen and Internet connection handy, fire it up and follow along as we journey into the past . . ."

[566] Says Spencer, "Who knew that 'VHS' stood for more than Very High Standards?"

1994

The first ball was cochaired by nurse Bobbie Jones and the honorable Lucy Coe. It featured these performances by the following:

- Dr. Kevin Collins, Dr. Monica Quartermaine, and Dr. Simone Hardy present "Triplets" from BANDWAGON

- Bobbie Jones and Dr. Tony Jones[567] dance the tango

- Dr. Steve Hardy recites "Casey at the Bat"

- Felicia Scorpio and Maxie Jones perform to "April Showers"

- Comedy by everyone's favorite funny guys, Jason Quartermaine[568] and his big brother A.J.[569]

- Further comedic stylings, this time from Mac Scorpio[570]

- Stone Cates and Robin Scorpio perform the death scene from the conclusion of ROMEO AND JULIET

---

[567] Editor's note: Dr. Jones failed to perform as scheduled. Damian Smith filled in at the last second when Tony's wife, Bobbie, was left without a partner.
568 Editor's note: Jason undertook this performance before the accident that would rob him of his memories and sense of humor.
[569] Editor's note: Reports vary as to the amount and sincerity of the laughter elicited.
[570] Editor's note: See above note.

Says Spencer, "The tango is an overrated dance. Clichéd and passé, it relies less on precision and good technique than on raw unquantifiable passion. As a performance piece, I vastly prefer a fine Viennese waltz. The Nae Nae is also good. The performance that most struck me was my beloved Emma's mother's[571] turn as Juliet. While I might take issue with the solemn tenor of the material,[572] the acting was impeccable and the effect was rousing. In fact, it has given me costume ideas for next Halloween. BUT SOFT, WHAT LIGHT THROUGH EMMA'S WINDOW BREAKS!"

Says Lucy, "In retrospect, Jason Morgan breaking smiles rather than bones makes this first Nurses Ball one for the ages. But no one who attended that ball wasn't moved by Robin and Stone's stirring performance of the tragic final scene from Shakespeare's classic play. They portrayed an urgency that belied their youth. I still remember Stone looking out at the audience and declaring, 'Shall I believe that unsubstantial death is amorous, And that the lean abhorred monster keeps Thee here in dark to be his paramour?' Stone and Robin would soon know exactly what monster Romeo spoke of.

[571] Robin Scorpio
[572] Says Spencer, "It's supposed to be a ball, not a burial."

1996

- This ball was cochaired by Katherine Bell and Lucy Coe. It featured performances by the following:

- Carly Roberts, Tony Jones, and Lucas Jones, who perform "Together" from GYPSY

- Dr. Alan Quartermaine, who sings "Beautiful Girls" from FOLLIES

- Ned Ashton, who sings "We're Having a Baby" from HOLLYWOOD CANTEEN

- Janis Tan, who performs WHEN ANGELS CRY

- Katherine Bell and Lucy Coe, who perform "Diamonds Are a Girl's Best Friend" from GENTLEMEN PREFER BLONDES

- Carly Roberts, Dr. Simone Hardy, Audrey Hardy, and Keesha Ward, who are featured in the finale "One" from A CHORUS LINE

Says Spencer, "I was tickled by Ms. Coe's spirited rendition of the song, and not because she told me I had to say that if I wanted to take part in this retrospective. Were I to produce this number today, I might consider turning the casting upside down and fiddle with the lyrics to remove some of the song's antiquated views on woman and lend the song a dash of local topicality. I'd call it, "Cassadines Are a Girl's Best Friend and Not Boys Named Cameron."

Says Lucy, "This ball was more poignant then pithy. Sonny Corinthos himself had allergies in his eyes when Janis Ian sang a tribute to lost friends. It was here that Sonny and the late Lily Corinthos donated $30 million dollars to establish the Stone Cates Memorial AIDS Wing. It was also here that Robin Scorpio made a courageous announcement that she contracted HIV, thus forcing everyone in that room to admit that they were now impacted by the disease as well. Mac Scorpio also presented Robin with a panel of the AIDS Quilt in honor of Stone, which is still on display today in General Hospital's atrium."

1998

This year's ball was chaired by Lucy Coe and underwritten by Stefan Cassadine. It featured performances by:

· Lucky Spencer, Dara Jensen, Elizabeth Webber, and Marcus Taggert, who perform JAILHOUSE ROCK

· Dr. Alan Quartermaine, Robin Scorpio, and Ned Ashton, who perform "Someone to Watch Over Me" from OH, KAY!

· Lucy Coe, Brenda Barrett, Dara Jensen, and Dr. Karen Wexler, who perform "Big Spender" from the musical SWEET CHARITY

· Eve Lambert and Julie Devlin, who sing "You've Got a Friend in Me" from TOY STORY

· Ned Ashton and Emily Bowen-Quartermaine, who sing THE POWER TO BELIEVE

· Scott Baldwin, Mac Scorpio, Edward Quartermaine, Serena Baldwin, Dr. Karen Wexler, Emily Bowen-Quartermaine, Robin Scorpio, and Maxie Jones, who sing "Thank Heaven for Little Girls" from GIGI and GIRLS JUST WANNA HAVE FUN

· Julie Devlin, Eve Lambert, and Karen Wexler, sing "One" from A CHORUS LINE

Says Lucy, "The next few years' worth of balls featured many memorable performances . . . and a few disasters as well. Literal disasters like a city-bound train crashing into a bus, and figurative disasters like Katherine Bell crashing into notes she couldn't handle. Then, like the rest of the world, the Port Charles economy couldn't support what many viewed as a frivolous expenditure."

Says Spencer, "Though as the ancient proverb goes, 'If you have only two pennies, spend the first on bread and the other on hyacinths for your soul.'"

Says Lucy, "The ball returned in 2013 after an anonymous donor[573] underwrote the entire thing."

disasters . . .
Literal
disasters

[573] Editor's note: Jerry Jacks, but who's counting?

2013

Hosted by Lucy Coe, the all new, all-different Nurses Ball featured performances by:

- Nurses Epiphany Johnson, Elizabeth Webber, Sabrina Santiago, and Felix DuBois, performing the opening number written and composed by Molly Lansing-Davis and T. J. Ashford, "Welcome to the Nurses' Ball"

- Damian Spinelli and Ellie Trout, performing "She Blinded Me with Science"

- Sam Morgan and Anton Ivanov dancing to "Jumptown Saturday Night"

- The ventriloquism[574] of Mac Scorpio[575] and his friend "Mister Marbles"[576]

- Frisco Jones singing "All I Need"

- Duke Lavery and Anna Devane dancing the tango[577]

---

[574] Says Frisco J, "And character assassination."
[575] Says Mac S, "Is it character assassination if it's true?"
[576] Says Frisco J, "If I ever see that puppet again, I'm going to turn it into kindling."
[577] Lucy's note: I was scheduled to dance with Duke but was, er, tied up by Richard "Jealous Much?" Simmons

- "Magic" Milo Giambetti, Michael Corinthos, Max Giambetti, Damian Spinelli, Anton Ivanov, and DuBois tearing off the roof and their clothes for a striptease

- Rick Springfield singing [578] "Jessie's Girl"

- Sabrina Santiago and Emma Scorpio-Drake performing "Call Me Maybe"

- Olivia Falconeri prognosticating as her alter ego THE BENSONHURST MEDIUM, with assistance from Max Giambetti

- Traction performing "Private School Girls" with Molly Lansing-Davis and T. J. Ashford

- Epiphany and the Revelations [579] performing "Jump"

- Sabrina Santiago and Dr. Patrick Drake closing the show with "You Are Not Alone"

---

[578] Says Olivia F-Q, "He was singing it straight to my heart."
[579] Dr. Monica Quartermaine and Tracy Quartermaine

Says Spencer, "I thought I read somewhere that that Simmons fellow was supposed to choreograph the opening number?"

Says Lucy, "We had to let him go. Creative differences."

Says Spencer, "Like they had in One Direction?"

Says Lucy, "Never you mind about that. What performance in that year was tops, Your Highness?"

Says Spencer, "Frisco Jones's grand romantic gesture won my heart—if not his ex-wife Felicia's. His courage in the face of his romantic rival, Mac, planted the seed for my own act's derring-do in the name of love. Speaking of Ms. Scorpio-Drake, her performance wondering if anyone would 'Call' her 'Maybe' was riveting—and my answer is yes, Emma, a thousand times yes!"

Says Lucy, "Though the year the Nurses Ball returned to General Hospital is a favorite for many, it was a low point for me, as I spent a goodly amount of it tied up. But I returned to the stage in time to witness Epiphany wail a treat then and a treat ever since."

2014

Hosted once again by Lucy Coe, performances included:

- Epiphany Johnson, Elizabeth Webber, and Felix DuBois opening the ball to Molly Lansing-Davis and T. J. Ashford's signature number, "Welcome to the Nurses' Ball"[580]

- Kiki Jerome, Elizabeth Webber, Lucas Jones, Felix DuBois, and T. J. Ashford performing "Raise Your Glass"

- Eddie Maine[581] performing "You Took the Words Right Out of My Mouth"

- Luke Spencer[582] performing "I Am What I Am" from LA CAGE AUX FOLLES

- "Magic" Milo Giambetti and His Magic Wands[583] stripping to "You Shook Me All Night Long"

- Blackie Parrish's performance of "Brokenhearted" being canceled due to a last minute scheduling snafu[584]

---

[580] Editor's note: The opening was interrupted and hijacked by Dr. Liesl Obrecht and a dance company performing "Willkommen" from *Cabaret* in a performance as appalling as it was captivating.
[581] Aka Ned Ashton
[582] Asks Lucy, "Was it Luke? Or Fluke? I'm still confused."
[583] Nathan West, Lucas Jones, Felix DuBois, Michael Corinthos, and T. J. Ashford
[584] Editor's note: Brad Cooper subbed in

- Ventriloquism from Mac Scorpio and his puppet, Mister Marbles [585]

- The Haunted Starlets [586] performing to the song "I Love It"

- Eddie Gomez singing "Criminal Love"

- Cameron Spencer and Emma Scorpio-Drake dancing the tango [587]

- Molly Lansing-Davis and T. J. Ashford singing "Just Can't Get Enough"

- Sabrina Santiago being scheduled to sing "Little Things" [588]

- Dr. Liesl Obrecht performing "Always on My Mind"

- Epiphany Johnson singing "You Are Not Alone"

[585] Says Epiphany J, "Don't worry, Frisco. I got your back that year. Mister Marbles was nothing but splinters when he left that ballroom."
[586] Sam Morgan, Maxie Jones, Molly Lansing-Davis, Lulu Spencer-Falconeri, and Kiki Jerome
[587] Their dance was interrupted by Spencer Cassadine with the band Player for a performance of "Baby Come Back"
[588] After Sabrina went into premature labor, Emma Scorpio-Drake took her place.

Says Lucy, "Spencer, this Ball was a big one for us both."

Sighs Spencer, "You're telling me."

Says Lucy, "I missed my cue when Scott and I were talking backstage."

Asks Spencer, "Do you always talk with your lips pressed together?"

Says Lucy, "Of course the curtain went up and we were caught talking. Kevin was not happy about that one."

Says Spencer, "My feelings about the tango are on record. The tango is over! No one should tango ever! Unless those tangoing are Emma Scorpio-Drake and myself! Then it's okay."

Asks Lucy, "How in the world did you get Player to perform?"

Says Spencer, "I acted boldly and beautifully."

Says Lucy, "I enjoyed the Magic Milo act. May those hunks of burning love always drop trou! I had no idea Sonny's bodyguard Milo packed a Magnum. Yet it Epiphany!"

2015

Hosted by Lucy Coe, this year's ball included performances by:

- Epiphany Johnson, Elizabeth Webber, Felix DuBois, and Sabrina Santiago opening the ball with the traditional number, "Welcome to the Nurses' Ball"

- Dr. Liesl Obrecht performing "99 Red Balloons"

- Ric Lansing singing [589] "Marry You" [590]

- Magic Milo and the Magic Wands [591] stripping to "New Sensation"

- The Haunted Starlets [592] performing to "Dear Future Husband"

- Cameron Spencer and Emma Scorpio-Drake dancing the tango [593]

---

[589] Editor's note: Ric intended this performance as a marriage proposal to Elizabeth Webber. In the midst of the song, Carly revealed Ric's duplicitous hiring of Hayden Barnes (who would later turn out to be Elizabeth's half sister by father Jeff Webber) to pretend to be the wife of Jake (who would later turn out to be Jason Morgan, only to later actually turn out to be Jason's identical twin Drew Cain) in order to keep him away from Elizabeth. Brad Cooper took over after Ric departed to salvage his relationship with Elizabeth. Brad sang an up-tempo rendition of the same song, in turn proposing marriage to Lucas Jones. Lucas said yes.

[590] Elizabeth declined. Says Lucy, "Never propose before an audience."

[592] Nathan West, Michael Quartermaine (Corinthos), T. J. Ashford, Lucas Jones, Felix DuBois

[592] Lulu Spencer-Falconeri, Maxie Jones, Sabrina Santiago, Sam Morgan, Ellie Trout, and Valerie Spencer

[593] This dance was once again cut short by Spencer Cassadine. Wearing a mask to encourage postburn healing, Spencer climbed into the rigging and dropped sandbags on the stage, nearly beaning the performers. Says Spencer, "Temporary insanity. I was mad with the grief of lost love."

- Patrick Drake and Emma Scorpio-Drake performing a duet to "Nothing I Can't Do"

- Eddie Maine singing "Crazy Little Thing Called Love", with backup from Epiphany Johnson, Felix DuBois, and Sabrina Santiago

- Damian Spinelli singing "It Might Be You"

- Epiphany Johnson and Sabrina Santiago singing "You Are Not Alone"

Says Lucy, "So much to say about this one, but age before beauty. Why didn't you let those two cuties finish their tango once again?"

Says Spencer, "Sometime you just gotta go pull a Phantom to get what you want."

Lucy: "That's the first time I've heard that word used as a verb."

Lucy Coe's
hosted ball;
2015

QUIZ TIME

When considering making the big move to Port Charles, you may want to first consider how you'll fit in here. I and my good friends at *Crimson* have put together the following quizzes to help you figure out your place in Port Charles.

QUIZ #1

WHAT GENERAL HOSPITAL HEROINE ARE YOU?

While in town, you might be looking for a local gal to show you the sights; this little quiz might help guide you and narrow down who would be your ideal hang.

What Kind of Clothing Are You Most Comfortable in?

a. Scrubs
b. Stilettos and chic dress
c. Jeans and motorcycle boots
d. A power suit

What Is Your Dream Job?

a. Artist
b. Owner of the chicest spots in the city
c. Talk show host
d. Supreme Court justice

What Is the Wildest Thing You've Ever Done?

a. Keep secret the knowledge that your presumed dead baby daddy is really alive
b. Try to pass off your baby's paternity . . . twice
c. Seduce your rival's husband, but split when he realizes you orchestrated the keeping of his son
d. Dress in drag as a male butler to spy on your ex's family

What's Your Drink of Choice at a Girl's Night Out?

a. Hot toddy; you like things cozy
b. Cosmo
c. Whatever is on tap
d. What's a girl's night out?

What Is Your Relationship With Your Extended Family Like?

a. Family is everything. Grams is your main source of support, and babysitting

b. Although you sought to destroy your birth mother, now you're besties

c. Your mother and sisters drive you crazy, but they're your pack. A newly found brother and father are trying to fit into the estrogen mix.

d. Nonexistent. Keep those crazies as far away as possible!

MOSTLY A's: *Elizabeth Webber.*
You're warm and caring, and your family and friends mean everything to you. However, your big heart often causes most of your problems.

MOSTLY B's: *Carly Corinthos.*
You're a businesswoman who knows what she wants and you usually get it. While those closest to you have your eternal loyalty, God help those who try to betray you or your family.

MOSTLY C's: *Sam McCall.*
Toughened by your difficult childhood, you revel in the family and love you found later in life.

MOSTLY D's: *Alexis Davis.*
You're a tough-as-nails attorney and pride yourself on your level head and belief in law and order. Unfortunately, your beliefs are often challenged by personal complications.

QUIZ #2
WHICH PORT CHARLES HUNK WOULD BE YOUR BAE FOR LIFE?

With so many hotties in the vicinity, we thought we'd help you find out who's a stud and who's a dud.

Choose a First-Date Activity.

a. A long ride on the back of a motorcycle

b. Learning to cook veal Parmesan in the kitchen of Pozzulo's

c. Get special permission to observe open-heart surgery at General Hospital

d. Go on a secret mission for the WSB

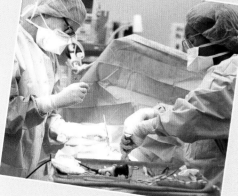

What's the Most Important Quality You Look for in a Guy?

a. Intense focus

b. Extreme loyalty

c. Analytic mind

d. Mystery

What Is an Ideal Anniversary Gift?

a. A sweater he saw you eyeing in a store window over a year ago and remembered to buy

b. Your own Caribbean island

c. Shares of ELQ stock

d. Being serenaded with a song he wrote just for you

If You Were in Trouble, Your Idea Man Would

a. Follow you to the depth of hell

b. Throw you a bulletproof vest and tell you to duck

c. Use his money and name to help you through it

d. Call a secret agent to help untangle the mess

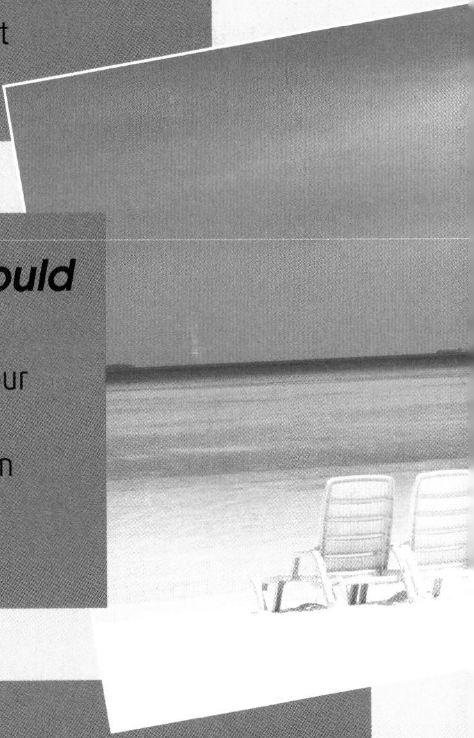

In His Free Time, Your Ideal Man Would

a. Stare longingly at you from across the room

b. Hang out on a secluded beach with you and your family

c. Write articles in medical journals that bring him world acclaim

d. Help save the world from outside threats

How Is Your Ideal Mate's Memory?

a. He crashed into a tree, so he has trouble with long-term stuff, but he's sweet in the short term

b. Like an elephant, he never forgets anything, even the times you might have married someone other than him

c. Good with the important stuff, like neurosurgery procedures, but sometimes not the best at remembering how many illegitimate children he might have

d. Pretty good, until he seems to forget the "till death do we part" bit

MOSTLY A's: *Jason Quartermaine.*
You like a man of few words, but your loyalty and love toward those you love is endless. Just make sure you have your helmet ready at all times because this "stone cold" mobster might ask you for a ride at any moment.

MOSTLY B's: *Michael "Sonny" Corinthos, Jr.*
You like a man who smells like a mixture of coffee and gunpowder. You have become a master at balancing fatherhood, love, and business. But sometimes maintaining your emotional highs and lows can be a challenge.

MOSTLY C's: *Alan Quartermaine.*
Your ideal guy belongs to an esteemed family, with all the money, power, and drama that comes along with that.

MOSTLY D's: *Frisco Jones.*
You like a guy who mixes espionage with musical stylings. Be prepared to be serenaded at the Nurses Ball, then whisked away on a secret mission.

QUIZ #3

WHAT ARE YOUR PORT CHARLES SURVIVOR SKILLS?

For a small hamlet we have had our fair share of disasters. See which one you'd be most likely to survive.

You've Been Committed to Shadybrook on the Belief That You're a Danger to Your Children (But You're Not Crazy YOU SWEAR). Do You:

a. Plead your case to your shrink

b. Seduce an orderly

c. Pick the lock with a paper clip

d. Hope Mac Scorpio will save you

You're Nine Months Pregnant and About to Give Birth. Which Nonideal Location Gives You and Your Baby the Best Chance for Survival?

a. A remote cabin where you are being held hostage by the woman who shot your son

b. A bomb threat has stalled your hotel elevator, in which you are stuck with the baby daddy who doesn't know he's the baby daddy

c. Alone in a dingy motel room with the nearest hospital a freezing cold hike away

d. On the bare floor of Port Charles's latest hot spot

Would You Rather Have

a. Dissociative identity disorder

b. Amnesia (at least twice)

c. A secret identical twin whose life you might have been living all along

d. A brain tumor that causes you to do terrible things

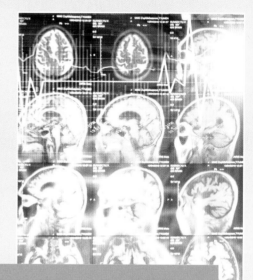

Your Penthouse Apartment Is on Fire and You Can Only Save One Item. Which One? (Your Kids Are Away, Visiting Their Dads, So They're Fine.)

a. The secret recipe to your grandma's tomato sauce

b. The adoption papers that list your birth parents, who you still haven't gotten around to contacting

c. Your ancient Aztec ring

d. The only known copy of Lila Quartermaine's secret diary in which she tells all

Would You Rather Attempt to Fight

a. The radiation from alien crystals from the planet Lumina

b. A horrific blizzard in the middle of the summer

c. A deadly pathogen in the water supply

d. Lassa fever

MOSTLY A's:
You'd survive the serial killer at the winter ball because you'd be cozied up in the coatroom with a Cassadine heir.

MOSTLY B's:
You'd survive the deadly carnival where a car plowed through the Whac-A-Mole with just a few rib contusions bandaged up by the hot new resident.

MOSTLY C's:
You'd be on board the *SS Tracy Quartermaine*, which sank in Port Charles Harbor, but would talk your way into the first lifeboat.

MOSTLY D's:
You'd survive being trapped in a cannery warehouse and coming face-to-face with your presumed dead first love.

QUIZ #4

WHICH PORT CHARLES VILLAIN ARE YOU MOST LIKELY TO FALL PREY TO?

In helping you best prepare for your visit here, I think it's only honest to tell you what to avoid, and in most cases, it's people. See for yourself by taking this quiz.

If a Friend Was Telling You They Were Going to Try to Stop Their Ex's Wedding, What Would Make You the Most Uncomfortable?

a. Planting a bomb in flowers

b. Kidnapping their child and erasing their memory

c. Pretending to be pregnant (it can happen for real quickly enough)

d. If they had plastic surgery so no would recognize them and they could plot in secret

Which Is the Worst Offense?

a. The potential release of nerve gas that could wipe out a whole town

b. Creating a weather machine that can control the whole world

c. Telling your lover that your baby died at birth, when you really sold him on the black market to pay some bills

d. Holding someone hostage while they are having a heart attack

Which Sounds Like the Best Option for Your "Final" Meal?

a. No food, just a cigarillo and a lighter

b. Oysters flown in from Greece

c. A BLT from Kelly's

d. A Kobe steak

Which Alias Do You Find the Least Threatening?

a. P. K. Sinclair

b. Who needs an alias? It's more fun for all to know one's misdeeds outright

c. Domino

d. The Balkan

What Do You Think Is Scariest?

a. Someone who threatens the world
b. Someone who threatens your family
c. Someone who questions reality
d. Someone who threatens their family (of which you just happen to be a member)

MOSTLY A's: *Cesar Faison.*
You are easily enticed by flowery prose, not to mention a disguise or two.

MOSTLY B's: *Helena Cassadine.*
Perhaps you have some mommy issues that have been left unattended for too long?

MOSTLY C's: *Heather Webber.*
Never one to question free food, you still might want to look around before a mysterious stranger sends you a milkshake or, especially, a BLT.

MOSTLY D's: *Jerry Jax.*
International charm will only take you so far. Be careful before you jump in the water; you never know what biotoxins might be lurking.

QUIZ #5

OF WHICH FABLED PORT CHARLES CLAN MIGHT YOU *(SURPRISE!)* FIND YOURSELF A MEMBER?

It happens to everyone. You get hit by a runaway prisoner transport vehicle hijacked by a convict bound for the chair despite her insistence that she was framed by the DVX, but your brother refuses to go under the knife because he blames you for his wife finding out that he suffused her hair dye with LSD in an effort to prove her unfit to parent their triplets, which *did* make her go nuts but also made her shoot the mayor in a dispute over a parking space, thus leading to her conviction and subsequent desperate bid for freedom in the very prisoner transport vehicle that ran you down! So there you are, languishing away in the hospital, skin sallow, eyes hollow, hair fallow—when in walks nurse Epiphany Johnson with startling news: the DNA test results confirm that your brother isn't your brother! Your mother isn't your mother! Your father isn't—well, you never knew your father, anyway, because your mother always said he was just some guy she met "passing through" on his way to Pine Valley! Nurse Epiphany *does*, however, know who your *real* family is—because their DNA happens to be all over GH's records. As she opens the envelope, you cast your mind back, poring over all the clues you ignored along the way. . . .

With Which Genetically Inherited or Predisposed Condition Have You Been (or Do You Continue to Be) Afflicted?

a. Beta-thalassemia. (Heck if I know what it is; it's all Greek to me.)

b. Bipolar disorder. (You're up, you're down, you're tearing around town, you can't get out of bed. . . .)

c. A non-life-threatening heart condition corrected by simple surgery. (Now, if only there was a correction for the moneygrubbing cockles of your heart.)

d. A predilection for hard living. (The bartenders around town all know your name, and everyone knows you've got a line on some Cuban cigars. . . .)

You're Locked In a Life-and-Death Struggle with Your Mortal Enemy. With Which Weapon Do You Strike the Mortal Blow?

a. A jewel-encrusted dagger that has tasted the blood of generations of your ancestors' enemies

b. Trick question! Your trusted enforcer would've dispatched any enemy of yours well before they could get within spitting distance.

c. Your sports car! You, in a one-on-one? And get blood on your Chanel suit? Puh-leaze. It's a shame about the dent, but surely there's a disreputable mechanic around who'll fix up your chassis as good as new.

d. A baseball bat. An ice chamber. A gun. A rigged parapet. Your own tart tongue. An improviser like you can make a weapon out of whatever's handy.

You've Been Wronged Most Grievously, and You Aren't One to Live and Let Live. How Do You Exact Your Revenge?

a. The old ways are the best ways. Put a curse on your adversaries and let the fates do the rest.

b. Don't overthink it. Ice the SOB.

c. Send them to the breadline with a boardroom bushwhack! They think they've got control of the company, but with your blackmail and bedroom skills you've mustered just enough votes to depose them and install yourself as CEO for life.

d. Living well is the best revenge! Despite your checkered past, you pull it together to save the world, get the girl, and become mayor! Enjoy life as the toast of the town whilst your rival withers away in a dead-end job railing about the unfairness of it all.

On the Subject of Real Estate, You Prefer . . .

a. Doric columns, secret passages, and seclusion. Island living is your bag.

b. Gotta have a gatehouse for your compound. It's all about defensible positions.

c. The grandest estate in town, big enough that each extended family has a wing to themselves. Yes, you'd prefer to have the place to yourself, but better to keep your enemies close . . . just not so close that you have to share a bathroom.

d. You've lived in a tent, in a boxcar, and under a bridge. Doesn't matter where you hang your hat, just so long as your true love is beside you when the stars come out.

MOSTLY A's: *Congratulations, You're a Cassadine!*

You hail from a mélange of Greco-Russian royalty, but don't bank on a long reign. Cassadines eat their young.

MOSTLY B's: *Congratulations, You're a Corinthos!*

Enjoy the fruits of your "coffee" empire while you can! The scuttlebutt from the DA's office is that indictments are a-coming. . . .

MOSTLY C's: *Congratulations, you're a Quartermaine!*

You were born with the greed gene and bicker with the best of them.

MOSTLY D's: *Congratulations, you're a Spencer!*

Tragedy is hot on your trail! But lucky you, you've got the grit and mettle to overcome everything life throws at you.

FURTHEI

While there's simply no better place to holiday or make a home than Port Charles, there are a few other locations of note that are an easy drive or scenic train ride away.

. . . right on the picturesque Llantano River . . .

LLANVIEW

Located on the Main Line outside Philadelphia, in Llantano County and right on the picturesque Llantano River, Llanview is a great place for a day trip. Home of the fabled newspaper, the *Banner*,[594] Llanview is fast becoming the communications capital of Pennsylvania. Adding to this reputation is the expansion of The Sun Media empire, run by Jessica Buchanan, who created the Sun News Channel.[595] Save time for a guided house-and-garden tour of famed homes such as Llanfair, La Boulaie, and the Buchanan estate. If you're hungry, I recommend grabbing a bite to eat at the Palace Hotel Restaurant or the Buenos Dias Café in the trendy, up-and-coming community of Angel Square.

[594] Editor's note: While the *Banner* was founded as a newspaper, it has in recent years gained a heavy online presence thanks to the efforts of Chief Operator Victoria Lord.

[595] Studio tours of the *Sun News Hour* set are available through advance booking.

PINE VALLEY

Upriver and not far from Llanview is the town of Pine Valley, founded in 1683 by frontierswoman Aggie Eckhardt. A number of corporations have relocated their headquarters to quaint Pine Valley, thanks to its low tax rate and proximity to urban centers. Industries there include Chandler Enterprises, Cortlandt Electronics, Enchantment Cosmetics, and Fusion Cosmetics. Fashionistas love Lacey's department store. I make it a point to drop in every year come Nurses Ball season to round out my wardrobe.[596] For lunch, grab a bucket of wings at the Cluck Cluck Chicken Shack. If the tour of Spoon Island floated your boat, check out Wildwind, an imposing mid-nineteenth-century manor, which gives Wyndemere a run for its money in the jeepers creepers department.

[596] Lucy's note: Don't tell Wyndham's!

CORINTH

If ghost tours are your thing, follow Luke Spencer and Holly Sutton's lead to Corinth, Pennsylvania. Once a thriving industrial town, Corinth became an international news story when its population was decimated by serial killer Gwyneth Alden. Luke guessed that Gwyneth "wiped out pretty much all of her friends and family in some twisted attempt to rid them of their pain. Better dead than in pain. I guess the woman never heard of Space Cakes." The Museum of Mayhem runs day trips to the Alden mansion as part of their "Death in the Country" interactive exhibit.[597]

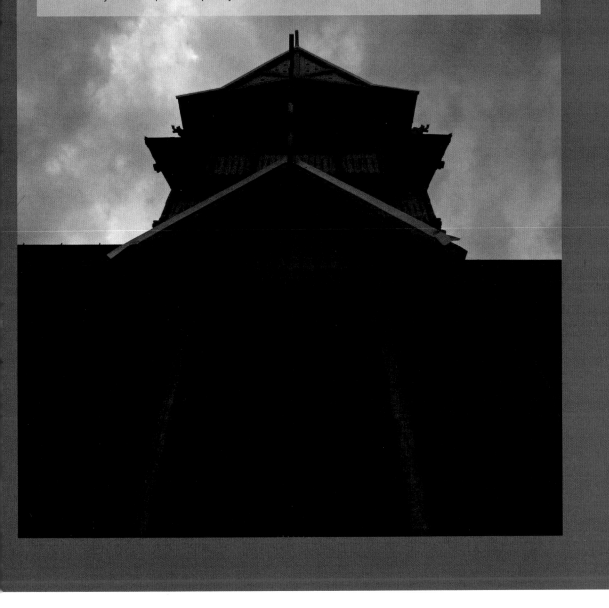

[597] Discount rates are available if you book both tours concurrently. Ask the concierge at the Metro Court Hotel for further details.

FINALE

Great secrets are hard to keep, but when they blow, they blow big. Like your friend's surprise birthday party, or the true identity of your unborn baby's father. The same is true of places like Port Charles. They might fly under the radar at first, but as soon as someone needs a cutting-edge face transplant, the secret is out! This shows everywhere in Port Charles—in the bustling waterfront, the expansion of our fine university, actual signs of expression on Jason Morgan's face! And while no one book can ever comprehensively capture the essence of a place,[598] I hope that this guide provides you with an impression of what Port Charles has to offer—and whom. As the late, great Mary Mae Ward once exclaimed, "Every single moment of our lives, whether born of joy or pain, has the potential for grace realized."

I believe Port Charles is a place where grace is realized every day—in the steps taken by children who've been thawed and reanimated; in the sight of the local police force paying tribute to one of their fallen; and in the bizarre yet deeply meaningful artwork hanging in the Jerome Gallery.

Still not sure? Come see for yourself. Use our guide to lead you to some of the more intriguing locations mentioned herein—then throw it away. Investigate. Explore. Every day I turn a corner and luck onto some surprising find or compelling character. Who knows—if you're intrepid enough, you just may luck onto

a sheltered cove on Spoon Island, tucked away from the madding crowd and mad Cassadines. But whatever you do, keep it on the DL—that's my secret spot for—. You'll know it when you scrabble over a cluster of boulders and spot a lone pine tree casting watch over the water. Come on the right day and you just may see a bunch of clothes hanging from the tree branches. Designer duds, of course, and a few skivvies. A bra—*not* a push-up.

WWW.CHUCKSLIST.ORG

While you're in Port Charles, make ample use of the Chuckslist website. Chuckslist started out as an informational pamphlet provided to new and visiting doctors and nurses and has since grown into a highly trafficked website that features advertisements for everything from short term waterfront rentals to the latest job openings in the Corinthos

---

[598] Spinelli says: "Actually I am currently working on a virtual reality device, complete with smell-o-vision, that will make travel and reading irrelevant."

Group.[599] One of its most popular features is the "Missed Connection" section. I used to get a good chuckle out of those ads; what kind of gullible hayseed eye makes eye contact over the rutabaga at the farmer's market and makes an instant, unfathomable bond? Then I met my doc. And though we're no longer together, I can't deny that it was our relationship that started me seeing the possibility in meeting your Mr. Darcy over pancakes down the counter at Kelly's. Here are a few of my favorite missed connection posts from over the years . . .

From an early archived issue: A rose is not a rose; it should instead be another flower . . . something lavender colored. I saw you walking in the park and haven't been able to get you out of my mind. I'd relish the opportunity to hear you recite a sonnet or two. Sincerely, more than a dime, less than a half-dollar.

---

[599] Lucy warns, "You'll make plenty of money working for Sonny; his jobs come with a lot of perks, but also high-hazard pay. Turnover is high.

To the boy in the leather coat, I saw you walking the docks and remembered the first time I bumped into you at the Nurses Ball. You weren't made of stone when we danced, and until you hit that tree, I never found you cold. Signed, a "Ward" of missed opportunity.

I was in line right behind you at the GH cafeteria. I wore scrubs; you had oil paint on your fingernails. You said the green in my scrubs brought out my eyes. I didn't know what to say. I'd spent the morning wrangling kids and administering IVs, feeling less than pretty. I wish I had time to talk, but I was in a hurry to pick up my kids and now I can't remember if I even said "thank you." Next time I see you, you'll fix that.

To the sad little man searching for his bride, it'll be an icy day in Hades before you find your princess. Though the devil knows better than to let us into his realm; we'd end up running the place. Not so fun to have your love taken from you, is it? Signed, The One Holding the Puppet Strings.

Dear Mob Princess, I'm missing your special brew. Sorry Mommy Dearest thinks I'm not the right person to teach you what you need to know. I promise you'll always get passing grades from me. Yours, the Nutty-for-you Professor.

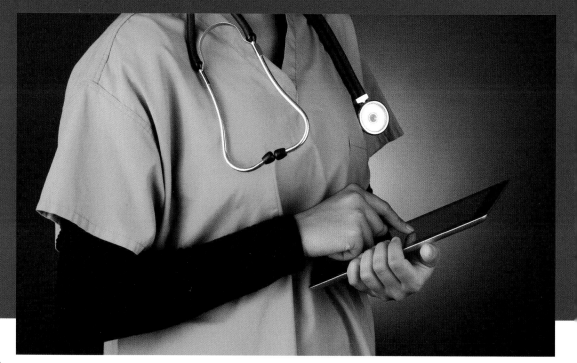

You said the green in my scrubs brought out my eyes